I0073890

The
Affordable Care Act
versus
Small Business

ENTREPRENEURS SURVIVING ACA

DR. IVAN J. SALABERRIOS

Pensiero Press

The Affordable Care Act Versus Small Business:
Entrepreneurs Surviving ACA

 Pensiero Press

Websites: www.ThePensieroPress.com | www.LentzLeadership.com
Twitter: https://twitter.com/drcheryllentz
Facebook: https://www.facebook.com/Dr.Cheryl.Lentz

All rights reserved. No part of this book may be reproduced or transmitted in any form or by any means, graphic, electronic or mechanical, including photocopying, recording, taping, Web distribution, or by any informational storage and retrieval system without written permission from the publisher except for the inclusion of brief quotations in a review or scholarly reference.

Books are available through Pensiero Press at special discounts for bulk purchases for the purpose of sales promotion, seminar attendance, or educational purposes. Special volumes can be created for specific purposes and to organizational specifications. Please contact us for further details.

Copyright © 2019 by Pensiero Press

Volume ISBN: 978-1-7329382-1-2
LAW009000   LAW / Business & Financial
*Kindle and electronic versions available

Cover design & production: Gary Rosenberg • www.garyarosenberg.com

Volume 1

*I dedicate this book
to the memory of my mother,
Aurea N. Garcia.*

Abstract

The Affordable Care Act (ACA) is arguably one of the most beneficial legacies of former U.S. President Barrack Obama. However, the Act presented hardships within the healthcare setting, as well as within the business setting. This text responds to the questions raised concerning whether ACA's good intent increased its adaptability in the healthcare and business professions to help advance the lives of Americans. As demonstrated herein, ACA impacts both large and small businesses in their detached and work-related levels. The pertinent question is whether the increasing push by the Trump administration to have ACA repealed and replaced emanates from the interpretation and understanding by business. Worth noting is that the sources researched during the writing of this book suggest proprietors prefer the traditional method of healthcare coverage.

However, different members of the U.S. Congress oppose and support the Act. The support and opposition to ACA seem to be along party lines, considering that majority Republicans oppose the Act while most Democrats support the Act. Changes are underway to repeal and replace ACA. Researchers indicated the Act affects small for-profit and non-profit organizations alike. This writing reveals how ACA massively impacts healthcare financial management. For instance, meeting the expanding consumer healthcare demand necessitates an increased rate of emerging ideas for universal healthcare. On this basis, this book includes recommendations of various strategies to help improve ACA rather than repealing the Act.

Contents

Testimonials

Richard Pembridge, Ed.D.
Acute Care Nurse Practitioner • Diabetes Center

Dr. Ivan Salaberrios presents the benefits and risks associated with the Affordable Care Act. The strategies present a compromising approach to balance the Affordable Care Act are primarily for the patients with chronic conditions and their challenges to affording *GOLD* standard care. When reading through this book, my initial thoughts for diabetes patients would be an approach to control cost instead of providing money to continue to pay the expenses associated with diabetes self-management. Dr. Ivan explains as a society and a country, political differences need to be put aside and focus on the market of disease management from a provider and manufacturer perspective.

Dr. Temeaka Gray
Women's Health Nurse Practitioner

In *The Affordable Care Act Versus Small Business: Entrepreneurs Surviving ACA*, Dr. Ivan Salaberrios provides an evaluation of the Affordable Care Act that delves into its impact on individuals, organizations, and governmental parties. His well-crafted analysis and strategies present an approach to balance between governmental parties that is no less than focused on *care*. I was drawn to consider the patients that I provide care for; those that for some reason or another would not have access to care without an agenda that puts aside differences in opinion and focuses on *care* of people simply because they are human, regardless of person views and experiences. This is a well written analogy of the health care world we live in with strategies that can provide a positive impact on the health care of America.

Gayle Bode

Bode Office Solutions • http://www.bodeoffice.com

I found this book to be insightful and packed with relevant details about the ACA and its effects on Small Businesses and worker's health. I saw a win, win, win scenario as Dr Salaberrios described the potential outcome from providing affordable health care to more people would result in higher demand for health care services as people use their newly obtained insurance coverage. This could add more small clinics in rural communities and increased demand for medical service and heath care jobs and opportunities nationwide. Benefits of enhancing and improving the ACA are outline here. Thank you Dr Salaberrios for your work.

Linda F. Patten

Leadership Trainer for Women Entrepreneurs and Changemakers–CEO, Dare2Lead With Linda • http://www.dare2leadwithlinda.com

The Affordable Care Act has been fraught with challenges throughout its history. This book is a comprehensive look at what the desired hopes and outcomes were when the Act was signed into law, compared to the realities today. As a former healthcare professional, I found it difficult to read about the unintended stresses the ACA has caused in today's healthcare arena. Among the issues Dr. Salaberrios outlines so clearly is the lack of healthcare providers to meet demand, and how small businesses have been adversely impacted, even as the consumer's healthcare costs have been lowered.

Dr. Ivan believes that solutions are possible, that the " . . . ACA deserves improvement rather than repealing." This clear-eyed, while sobering, book needed to be written, and I'm grateful that Dr. Ivan has so competently tackled this complex subject which touches all of our lives, and future lives, in some way.

Dr. Elmer Hall, DIBA, MBA
President, Strategic Business Planning Company •
http://ipplan.com/

Dr Ivan does a great job of talking us through the healthcare system we currently have, the ACA or Obama Care system. Understanding the history and political lines is important but solving the healthcare issues is critical and needs to rise above politics. Healthcare is so important that everyone must rise above the dogma of party lines and focus on real solutions. Health and wellness is critical to well-being and the pursuit of happiness, but from and economic point of view, healthcare costs can, and will bankrupt the nation. Healthcare as a percent of GDP had ballooned at 10% per year for decades, from 6% in mid-1900s to about 18% of GDP today. The Great Recession, expiring drug patents and–to some extent, at least, the ACA–have lowered the rate of healthcare cost increases to a mere 4%. That is still twice the rate of inflation, but not a problem that will bankrupt the nation in 10 to 20 years. Good work Dr. Ivan, thanks for a prescription to the ailing healthcare system.

Acknowledgments

I want to thank my wife, Charlotte M. Hughes, for supporting me throughout my career. My children Gabrielle B., Alexis T.N., Aquil J., Aurea I., Justin M., and Alyssa M. Salaberrios for inspiring me to do my best for you. Thanks to my father Miguel A. Salaberrios for being my role model and setting a high standard for a man's work ethic.

Special thanks to my editor and mentor Dr. Cheryl Lentz. Thanks to The Refractive Thinker® series for allowing me to contribute to such a fine academic journal. Thank you to the publisher, Pensiero Press, and to graphic designer Gary Rosenberg.

CHAPTER 1

Introduction

The Affordable Care Act (ACA), popularly known as Obamacare, is a contemporary business and healthcare issue warranting divergent opinions. The Act is arguably a breakthrough in reform legislation regarding health care in the United States. Passed by the members of the 111th U.S. Congress and later signed into law by President Barack Obama in 2010, the Act contains an extensive list of healthcare related provisions aimed at extending or offering coverage to millions of the uninsured Americans. The objectives include expanding healthcare insurance access and protecting people from overwhelming medical debts. However, many seem interested in knowing whether this good intent makes providing health insurance any more manageable for small businesses.

The main aim of the Act was to lower health care costs, eliminate the recession, and ensure those with pre-existing conditions have insurance coverage. These objectives included improving the efficiency of the healthcare system with these three primary goals. Following its enactment, 32 states expanded Medicaid coverage to adults in low-income America since 2010. However, 19 States are yet to expand Medicaid coverage to adults. In 2018, President Donald Trump declared his commitment to ensuring that Obamacare is repealed; he seems to be getting closer that dream. Since its establishment in 2013, ACA remains at the center of contemplation with numerous impacts on small businesses in America. This book includes discussion of the possible impacts of Obamacare on the healthcare organization in the United States from a business perspective.

There are three primary goals of the Act. First, the Act seeks to make health insurance affordable and available to more people including individuals in low-income households. The Act provides varying subsidies to consumers aimed at lowering the costs incurred in healthcare. The subsidies included in the Act are the premium subsidies, as well as cost-sharing subsidies. These two subsidies help minimize the costs of health coverage for all Americans who qualify. Second, the Act helps expand programs such as Medicaid that cover all adults with an income below 138% of the U.S. federal poverty level. However, evidence suggests that not all the states expanded their Medicaid programs as required by the Act. Third, the Act targets low-income households with the objective of supporting any medical care related innovation that can potentially minimize costs incurred in health care at all levels. ACA was aimed at helping the poor families spend less on the health insurance premiums and out-of-pocket care.

ACA brings accountability in the insurance market by prohibiting bad insurance industry practices that for years made it impossible for millions of Americans to access and afford health coverage. Before the Act was implemented, health insurance premiums rose rapidly without any explanation from the insurers. Raising health insurance premiums strains the budgets of American small businesses and families. However, following the implementation of the Act, insurers have been barred from dropping Americans' insurance coverance. The Act brought an unprecedented level of transparency and scrutiny to the health insurance by requiring health insurance companies to justify any increase in the health insurance rates before they reflect on the bill of Americans. Consequently, the Act prevented the unnecessary or arbitrary costs. The purpose of the Act is to guarantee more choices for the quality of health care to Americans. The Act affords individuals many benefits to include: free preventive care; coverage for pre-existing conditions, rebates from insurance companies, coverage of young adults who are under the age of 26, and no cancellations or lifetime limits on care. The Act includes preventive guidelines aimed at ensuring every qualified person stays healthy, as well as ensuring members access health care services when needed.

CHAPTER 2

Background

A choice analysis constitutes an integral part of policy formulation and in particular policies that affect a population or residents of a particular nation. In the case of ACA, the incorporation of the same procedures used in the program scrutiny helped create comprehensive policies. These involved determining the dimension of choice for policymakers. Legislators seeking alternatives to ACA that could be considered cost-effective accomplished this objective. An array of questions, notably the bases of social allocations, govern the aspects of choices. In the case of ACA, the bases of social allocation addressed the beneficiaries and the policies passed by the U.S. Congress. ACA stipulates eligibility and the extent to which members include entitlement to the policy. As indicated, the beneficiaries of OBAMA care are the low-income householders. The Act stipulates the benefits enjoyed by these low-income households and offers an objective view than previous Acts did. The Affordable Insurance Exchanges contained in the Act provides the eligibility policy that stipulates coverage for low-income households. These eligibility policies have a minimum stipulated Medicaid income level eligibility level across all states.

Worth noting is that as defined by the Act, choice is a form of the benefit received independent of whether in the form of cash, power, or vouchers. The nature of social provision allocated by the policies varies depend on whether the U.S. government provides the low-income households with better facilities and assure no hindrance in the acquisition of the healthcare services. The legislature intended to find alternative forms of provisions, including power and vouchers that can act as vital social provisions allocated to help meet the primary goals of ACA.

The third aspect of ACA addresses the strategies for the delivery of healthcare provisions. The aspect explicates the provision of services how consumers are organized. In the plans addressed by ACA, the consumers and the providers are well-organized in ways that sanction cohesion, legality, and development. These types of coordination make ACA stand out from other healthcare programs. In analyzing ACA, the fourth important aspect is the mode of financing, separated into two sections. The first section sheds light on the sources of capital, while the second section gives insight into the systems of transfer of funds. The newly eligible individuals covered by ACA included full funding by the U.S. federal government since the beginning of 2014 for approximately 3 years.

Events Leading to the Introduction of the ACA

ACA introduced changes aimed at addressing the shortcomings of the Social Security Amendment Act, signed by President Lyndon Johnson in July 1965. This Act of 1965 created the landmark Medicare program, providing for individuals aged 65 and older with hospital insurance and medical assistance. In an attempt to make health care services available, the amendment created the Medicaid program designed for individuals deemed incapable of affording health care insurance. The Act used the Social Security Amendment Act as a basis to suggest changes that would see the low-income earners afford healthcare.

While signing into law the Social Security Amendment Act, President Johnson stated:

> No longer will older Americans be denied the healing miracle of modern medicine. No longer will illness crush and destroy the

savings that they have so carefully put away over a lifetime so that they might enjoy dignity in their later years. No longer will young families see their incomes, and their hopes eaten away simply because they are carrying out their deep moral obligations to their parents, to their uncles, and their aunts.

President Johnson's statement echoed for many generations. Before then, all efforts to create vigorous national health insurance were unsuccessful. For instance, President Roosevelt and Harry Truman made several attempts to push for health reforms by targeting national health insurance. President Kennedy attempted to address the problem advocated for the Medicare in 1962. These attempts did not come to pass. Later, President Johnson advanced the advocacy and worked to overcome the fierce opposition from many critics including doctors, as well as the Democrats.

The Medicare program remains a landmark program in the healthcare sector because of its profound impact that eventually changed the provision of care to Americans. The Medicare program allowed the U.S. federal government to play a significant role in the health care system in the United States. The U.S. government proved this strategy was a significant boost for future reforms, addressing various problems faced by those who could not afford medical care because of the lack of insurance.

President Clinton made another attempt to create healthcare programs aimed at addressing the problem. Clinton made attempts to expand federal healthcare under the Clinton Health Care Plan. Clinton sought to develop universal health care for all Americans. These attempts saw them introduce the Health Security Bill to the U.S. House of Representative but failed to pass the U.S. Senate. Later, President George W. Bush signed into law the most significant expansion of the Medicare program: the $400 Billion Medicare Prescription Drug Modernization Act, becoming the basis for the creation of Obamacare. The Act enabled all Medicare recipients to afford prescription drugs. The Medicare Prescription Drug Modernization Act provided billions of dollars in subsidies to health maintenance organizations and insurance companies by allowing private plans to compete with the Medicare program. The Act permitted the importation of drugs from Canada with the approval of the FDA. The move reduced the unaffordability and inadequacy of drugs. However, worth noting is that similar to Obamacare, this Act faced opposition from the Republicans.

Next, efforts during the era of President Obama brought reforms aimed at addressing the problem faced by individuals who could not afford medical insurance health care. These efforts saw the introduction of the Patient Protection and Affordable Care Act. The Act required Americans to obtain insurance and imposed a penalty for those who did fail to do so. The Act prohibited insurance companies from discriminating people based on their pre-existing medical conditions with a mandatory requirement for the companies to offer primary essential benefits. Those against the legislation were from conservatives and members who hailed from the Tea Party Movement in their respective districts.

Changes After the Introduction of ACA

This section includes discussion of the history of the problem of the inability to afford health insurance and some of the factors that helped the Democrats to propose changes in the Act. During his campaign in 2008, President Obama insisted on the creation of necessary reforms to the health care system claiming that the cost of health care was a threat to the American economy. He indicated that health care had to be a right for every American. After assuming office, the president implored upon the U.S. Congress to pass reforms aimed at making health care affordable to every American.

ACA took effect after many attempts to halt through the courts. ACA protects American patients from any abuse by the insurance companies, expanding Medicaid and Medicare. The Affordable Care Act efficiently addressed the problems faced by low-income and middle-income families, addressing past shortcomings of previous attempts. With continuing implementation of the program, challenges abound. Currently, not all states implemented the reforms to help expand Medicaid.

ACA impacts both large and small corporations. It is important for business owners to know the potential risks because ACA provides all workers access to health insurance. Small business owners have a wrong perception towards ACA by assuming that ACA's design is for large businesses or those with 100 and above full-time workers. Any confusion largely contributes to the lack of understanding of ACA's designation of a full-time employee included full-time equivalent (FTE) employees. Worth emphasizing is that part-time, seasonal, and leased employees are also FTE employees. ACA provides for a complicated calculation for employers to calculate the total number of hours FTE workers spend. ACA excludes seasonal workers which small businesses may exploit to keep its seasonal employees out of the calculation to reduce their expenditure on healthcare insurance.

CHAPTER 3

Legal Hurdles

Since signed into law, ACA has withstood and endured numerous legal hurdles beginning in 2013. For instance, legal issues in ACA between March 2010 and June 2012 caused riveting political drama. The Act acquired support from the U.S. federal courts contrary to decisions of the Supreme Court that upheld the landmark law. One decision surprised most pundits and politicians as they expected a direct partisan outcome. However, Chief Magistrate John Roberts, together with four other moderates to liberal justices, joined hands and upheld the significant parts of health reforms. In his explanation, Roberts stated that they did not consider whether the Act embodied sound policies because that is a judgment entrusted to the elected leaders of the nation. Roberts added that the court only asked whether the U.S. Congress has the mandate under the U.S. Constitution to pass the challenged provisions.

The court tossed the troublesome Act back into the partisan and electoral field. Notably, all the legal fights were arguably along the partisan lines all along. The U.S. Supreme Court ruling in 2012 never eliminated the attempts to force the courts to do what politicians failed to do, which was to repeal ACA. While, the political fight over health reforms remains front and center, opponents of the changes transformed legal challenges. Surprisingly, the opponents went back to the Supreme Court in the King v. Burwell case in 2015. Because the Supreme Court settled the constitutionality of the law in 2012, the opponents aimed at its funding whereby they challenged the delivery of tax subsidies to millions of

Americans who took part in state exchanges instituted by the U.S. federal government.

The seemingly literal and palpable reading crumbled because of the weight of the well-established legal guidelines and precedents. Previously, courts decreed that laws ought to be interpreted according to their overall aim. Therefore, it is wrong to focus on just a few words taken out of context. The court decision in June 2015 was unusually strong when the six Supreme Court Justices established that ACA always mandated for subsidies to be accessible in all 50 states in the country. By doing so, the court raised the bar for conservative challenges in the future. Also, the court did not say that the policymaking branch provided universal subsidies by merely delivering its interpretation of a vague provision. Instead, the majority in the court ruled that the U.S. Congress always had the intention that subsidies provided to states depended on federal exchanges. Also, the court ruled that the subsidies should benefit the states that built their exchanges as well. Hence, the court solved the issue in accordance with the law.

Despite push and pull regarding the U.S. Congress's chaos while writing and proofreading the ACA text, the 2015 Supreme Court ruling terminated the challenger's focus and misquotation of the four words. After long precedents, the majority in the Court looked at the law and identified the universal availability of subsidies was necessary for ensuring insurance affordability in functioning insurance markets. The court noted that without subsidies, insurance markets in most states were likely to go into a *death spiral*, which could not have been the U.S. Congress's intention. The threat of a death spiral seems to settle the legal challenge to ACA. By legally challenging health reforms through the right-wing opponents, political strategists made attempts to convince partisans and worried voters that health reform is dangerous and uncertain. Opponents attracted the attention of the media to influence public perception and instigating a grassroots' resistance.

While the Republicans lamented the Supreme Court's 2015 ruling, the ruling saved the GOP from a win-lacking explosion that challengers attempted to ignite by denying millions of Americans their insurance benefits. Lawmakers argue that if the court could rule to the contrary and cut off the subsidies, many Americans would have lost access to affordable private health plans in states such as Florida, Texas, and Ohio. Important why specifically in these states?

CHAPTER 4

Ethical Perspective on ACA

One of the objectives of ACA is to assure all Americans access to health care regardless of their age, race, gender, socio-economic status, and medical history (Manchikanti et al., 2017). However, the Act addressed numerous ethical issues in the business and healthcare settings. This chapter uses the theories of normal functioning and distributive justice and the four standard ethical principles (i.e., principlism) to argue and justify the right to healthcare as reflected in ACA.

Collaborative Care Model

The Collaborative Care Model, an integrated health system established by Katon & Unützer, (2013), highlighted the potential ethical pitfalls of ACA. The model details the process of screening patients for psychiatric conditions in a primary care setting, through the help of simple rating scales. If the screening shows positive results, the patient visits a care manager, in most cases a behavioral health provider, to supervise their psychiatric care. In turn, the care manager is under a psychiatrist's supervision, whose role is to review cases regularly but does not visit the patient unless under unusual situations. The measurement of patient progress occurs using rating scales to the point of achieving clinical goals. As such, the physicians receive payment based on the clinical results.

Despite the reported success, the Collaborative Care Model poses numerous ethical questions. Before moving forward, understanding the relationship between the model and ACA is imperative. Some care models proposed by ACA encompass specialty psychiatric care offered by non-specialists, such that a psychiatrist only has limited contact with the patient. Moreover, ACA's value-based provision involves the payment for performance in relation to the U.S. federal tenets that might not reproduce quality care to patients in actual practice. The health coverage for all is a development that might drive patients to an already problematically low number of psychiatrists. Therefore, some loopholes from which the ethical issues emanate, especially for psychiatrists who care for private pay patients only. Note that the typically considered cardinal medical ethics principles are four. These are:

1. Autonomy

2. Justice

3. Beneficence

4. Non-maleficence.

The Belmont report identifies principles of autonomy, justice, non-maleficence, and beneficence as constituting the standard ethical principles for analyzing ethicality of clinical issues in healthcare (Emanuel et al., 2008). Brock (1995) argued that these four principles can be used to discuss and frame practical moral problems. These principles serve as federal law's supporting beam, widely used to guide the moral concern and ethical issues in medical practice.

Principle of Autonomy

The debate on the right to healthcare has dominated the American media and political sphere for decades. The debate tends to incline towards the distributive healthcare with proponents of right to healthcare using distributive justice as a justification of access to right to access healthcare (Daniels, 2007). Daniels (2007) argued that healthcare is of moral importance because of facilitating the preservation of normal functioning of the society leading to happiness, welfare, and opportunity. This chapter combines the *principlism* and the arguments in favor of the right to healthcare to justify the right to healthcare as provided in ACA.

With regard to autonomy and human right, Andorno (2009) suggested that the discussion on the expansion of healthcare coverage using federal funding should include the reasons of human rights and dignity. Andorno continued to note people intend to use healthcare as it is designed. It is important to demonstrate the value of human beings and the relevance of healthcare to all Americans. It is worth emphasizing that every human being has an intrinsic value and preserving human rights means preserving human dignity and the respective the intrinsic value of the entire humanity (Andorno, 2007). Human dignity relies on the interpretation from the spiritual dimension (Andorno, 2007). One cannot gain human dignity by achievement or labor. This term simply means that humans naturally inherit rights to sustain a living. Human dignity means protecting human life, freedom, and property as well as protection against unequal treatment and oppression (Beauchamp & Childress, 2009). These arguments suggest that a country committed to promoting human dignity must focus on promoting equal access to healthcare with the aim of eliminating illnesses that threatens to disrupt health of its citizens (Ruger, 2010). That means guaranteeing medical goods and services to all citizens with a view to promoting and sustaining their existence regardless of religion, race, and social-economics (Ruger, 2010).

Christian theory argues that life is sacred (Kelly, Magill, & Have, 2013). The argument is that the sacredness of human life lies in its integrity, destiny, and dignity and that human beings participate in God's holiness and created in the image of God (Kelly et al., 2013). The recognition of the importance and sanctity of human life by Christians justifies the support towards the provision of *quality of life* and implies the rightness to use health care services to preserve human life. The recognition of the sanctity of human life emphasizes the importance of preservation of the lives of the rich and the poor without partiality. The governments' responsibility for considering the quality of each human life but not necessarily advocating for the provision of unlimited resource to everyone (Ashley, 1982).

Others argued that justification of the right to healthcare encompasses the freedom to self-rule and personal autonomy (Beauchamp & Childress, 2009). It is also argued that an autonomous person enjoys the freedom from limitation of making personal and preferred choices and from another people's control (Beauchamp, & Childress, 2009). Personal autonomy means an individual has the freedom to execute the self-chosen plan and strategy and act based on own values without due interference from others. Aristotle (1962) captures this view with a perspective on personal autonomy. Aristotle states that humans act by a choice not generated from an outside force rather from the inner personal force. Personal autonomy means that an individual has the natural free will to act. Immanuel Kant (2010) explained human autonomy entails allowing a moral agent to own actions performed. Kant further argued that a responsible agent must choose freely and that choosing freely means being autonomous. Describing a concept of autonomy in making choices and human determination is relevant when it comes to individuals making decisions regarding health care choices. Emphasizing the importance of considering the value of health care and making decisions to access it without other people's controlling interference (Beauchamp & Childress, 2009). The before mentioned is the concept of autonomy as used within the context of healthcare. In contrast, individuals who cannot make decisions such as persons with retardation and prisoners lack autonomy while controlled by others. The health care sector denies individuals the liberty in autonomy by offering inadequate health care services (Beauchamp & Childress, 2009).

Others argued that through self-governance, Americans can manage their decision on healthcare and other issues that touch on their life (Beauchamp & Childress, 2009). The principle of respect for personal autonomy requires an individual's right to make decisions based on personal values and a right to self-respect. Daniels (2008) suggested allowing people the freedom to make choices regarding cost of healthcare from their physical condition regardless of their health or disability status. Within the context of health care, self-governance means respecting individuals' freedom to access healthcare services based on personal choices and wishes (Kass, 1990), to the extent that it becomes obligatory for physicians to help patents in making sound medical decisions that would enable them to overcome medical impediments and other obstacles (Katz, 1984). Even autonomous individuals who self-govern their health may have constraints caused by coercion, depression, illness and other conditions that limit their options (Beauchamp & Childress, 2009). One of the conditions that may limit people's options is not getting healthcare service when they fall sick. In most individuals, illness creates causes physical suffering and creates the desire to seek treatment. Respect for autonomy entails maintaining individual's autonomous choices and eliminating conditions that threaten or destroys autonomous action. On the contrary, disrespect of autonomy entails ignoring people's autonomous choices (Beauchamp & Childress, 2009). The failure to provide treatment to Americans examples the actions that disrespect autonomy.

ACA addresses the autonomy and human right in several ways. For example, the Act ensures American enrollees of Medicaid and Medicare access to information about their rights to receive medical care services to make decisions whether to refuse or accept treatment (Sandar, 1990). The provision protects the use of physician principle of non-maleficence as well as provides patients' autonomous right. ACA policy applies to health plans and institutional providers that participate in Medicaid and Medicare. These include home health care providers, hospitals, health maintenance organizations, nursing homes, and hospices.

ACA guarantees health service to every American by requiring Americans to commit to tax contribution as a demonstration that they understand their obligation to facilitate the country achieve the goal of ensuring everyone has the right to health. In addition, ACA assures affordable and quality health care to all Americans. The Act prohibits annual or lifetime limits of participants' benefits with the aim of improving health care coverage (Grossman, Sterkx, Blount, & Volberding, 2010). ACA sets out minimum health care insurance coverage for evidence-based services, such as screenings and immunization practice for children and infants, breast cancer screening for women. The ACT offers services under the guidelines of Health Resources and Services (Grossman et al., 2010). These guidelines make certain that services follow evidence-based research recommendations and all Americans receive quality care regardless of their employment status and income level (Grossman et al., 2010). Furthermore, ACA measures, including prevention and wellness programs, stress management, weight management, nutrition, physical fitness, diabetes prevention, health lifestyle support, and heart disease prevention; focus on ensuring health services are available to all Americans, as well as to promote general health. Importantly, ACA policies are in line with moral rules by defending rights of others. These ACA policies do not restrict health services based on financial ability, employment status, and health status.

Non-Maleficence and Beneficence

The lack of health care coverage to a large proportion of Americans ignites a discussion regarding the right to receive treatment.

Beneficence requires individuals to engage in actions that benefit the welfare of others. Beneficence is associated with acts of humanity, charity, kindness, and mercy (Beauchamp & Childress, 2009). Morality demands that people do good unto others. The principle of beneficence emphasizes the moral obligation by a person to act in a way that benefits others. The principle of beneficence applies when providing healthcare access to Americans who may not be able to afford it. The moral theory emphasized the obligatory actions to remove and prevent harms, consider harms and goods of an action and give benefit.

The moral right to access healthcare by all Americans supports fair and equal opportunity to all Americans in society. The right to access healthcare can be achieved through government-funded health services (The Library of Congress Thomas, 1990). A view which suggests the need for national health policy in the U.S. A national health policy that may guarantee the care to diagnose, treat disease, prevent illness, improve health conditions or disability, and treat injury associated with avoidable mature mortality and morbidity (Ruger, 2010). ACA includes such points.

Justice

Based on the principle of justice, equal treatment should be given to all Americans based on equitable, appropriate, and fair distribution of social goods (Ruger, 2010). Medical ethics define healthcare as a social good. Moral justification requires that medical services should be distributed because of wellbeing (Powers & Faden, 2006). The two perspectives support the goal of offering health services to all Americans based on justice. Most theories of justice support the distribution of healthcare to all as a social good. These theories of justice emphasize the principles of equal need and share. Theories of justice concerned with healthcare such as the Rawls' (1971) theory of justice tend to advance their arguments based on the need base. For example, federal and local government distribute welfare assistance, unemployment subsidies, and other public health programs on an as-needed basis. This approach of distributive justice, based on need, presumes the governments provide basic needs sustain living. Such an approach assumes healthcare is a basic need (Dougherty, 1988).

Without healthcare, Americans may have a shortened life. This theory prompted the Obama administration to recommend the provision of decent minimum healthcare services. Daniels and Sabin (2002) reflects the administration's view that justice is fairness and based on the Rawls' (1971) theory of Justice as fairness, opportunity should be protected to ensure that each person can obtain a fair share of opportunity range. Daniels and Sabin further advanced that Americans shall embrace a just healthcare system based on the *fair equality of opportunity* principle. In this argument, Daniels and Sabin considered a just healthcare system as encompassing an arrangement of healthcare distribution that provides a fair share of opportunities to each person in the society to pursue life goals. A just healthcare system corrects disadvantages and eliminate factors that hinder the fair access to equal opportunities. Societal challenges and illness are typical examples of barriers that prevent people from pursuing life goals. Both societal challenges and illness put restrictions on individuals' opportunity to life goals. In line with this view, equal access to healthcare by all Americans is important to help the country to achieve, restore, and maintain the functioning of the society by preventing illness, injury, and treatment.

ACA has programs that address the healthcare justice: the Medicare and the Medicaid programs. The U.S. elderly population is eligible for Medicare. ACA made improvement in the Medicare program by establishing the Center for Medicare & Medicaid Innovation (CMI). CMI allows analytical and clinical experts with expertise in health care management and medicine to conduct research. The research tasks CMI with testing service delivery models and innovative payment with a view to controlling cost and ensuring quality of care is delivered. ACA improved Medicare by allowing the use of bonus payments to assess the insurer's level of care management and care coordination (Grossman et al., 2010). Furthermore, ACA improved on the Medicare prescription drug by creating the 50% health insurance coverage gap discount for Part D enrollees' brand-name medications. The Act expanded the standard Part D benefit by $500 (Grossman et al., 2010). The arrangement was intended to deliver quality healthcare to the U.S. elderly population at a reduced out-of-pocket cost through public health programs. The effort distributes healthcare resources to Americans who may not be able to financially afford them. Thus, the program satisfies justice's demand for distributive healthcare. It is worth emphasizing that the older population tends to have lower financial means and health issues that create high demand for healthcare services (Daniels, 1988). Medicaid guarantees the elderly adequate health care services that protects their opportunity and functioning. By providing them with Medicaid, the U.S. government shows appreciation to the elderly by recognizing past efforts and contributions made in the society by the elderly citizens. This way, the U.S. government applies the distributing justice principle by demonstrating that all persons pass through similar stages of life and they should receive same treatment.

Justice for health is demonstrated in ACA's expansion of the Medicaid program, which is targeted at the disabled and poor population. ACA expanded the eligibility for Americans with lower income. The Act expanded the eligibility for Medicaid program for all, children, childless adults, and parents not eligible for Medicare.

The Act meets the requirement for justice by ensuring the disadvantaged and poor population receive equal resources. ACA's qualifying criterion requires Americans with family income below or at 133% of federal poverty line to receive equal resources. The Act strengthens the program by providing that federal medical assistance to fund the cost of covering enrollees eligible to Medicaid (Grossman et al., 2010). ACA provides for the simplified Medicaid and CHIP enrolment and improve Medicaid quality for providers and patients, as well as offers new options for long-term supports and services. This way, the Act offers enhance federal support to the poor. Intentionally, ACA provides plans for improving the delivery and quality of care for Medicare and Medicaid participants. ACA recognizes that justice demands embracing interventions that prevent nocuous consequences and remedy disadvantage condition (Powers & Faden, 2006). The Act recognizes that the disabled and poor Americans are full moral agents entitled to equal respect. Poor and disabled Americans are often stigmatized, and their well-being negatively affected. Poor and disabled Americans are unlikely to improve their health without the support of others or the government. A lack of health resources places the poor and disabled at a higher health risk, and subsequent shorter life expectancy. The detrimental consequences equally affect children in low-income families ("The Bellagio Study", 2003). Poor and disabled Americans have reduced chances to pursue life goals.

CHAPTER 5

Social, Economic, and Political Analysis of ACA

The consequences of ACA reforms are the most significant driver so far in regard to the ethical nature of ACA. The moral nature of the law supports the mandate to promote justice, solidarity, and ultimately the best common good. Regarding justice, ACA supports a fair distribution of critical social goods and offers the same or equal economic growth for all Americans. The law warrants Americans access health care at an affordable cost and that citizens have equal access to insurance. The goal of The Affordable Care Act is to improve the quality of care (Manchikanti et al., 2017). Economically, ACA makes certain every American has equal opportunities for growth and that all the opportunities presented to them are the same. The solidarity, a form of social justice, by contrast, gives a sense of togetherness, which in turn prompts Americans to be of assistance to one another during the time of need. ACA ensures that the society flourishes and that every member has the same chance to thrive, as well as providing that no one prospers more than the other. Thus, ethically and regarding social and economic justice, the Act maintains integrity. The current reforms do not create gaps. However, if Congress approve the amendments proposed by the current U.S. Congress and President Obama's government, then a considerable difference will emerge between *social* justice and *economic* justice.

Social Analysis

Socially, the Act of 2010 signifies the most significant reform in U.S. health care. The changes were put in places to address the problems regarding health care and the quality of the services rendered (Manchikanti et al., 2017). In such a case, therefore, the goal was to increase access to health insurance for all Americans, which was not the case previously, especially among those with pre-existing conditions or those who were below the poverty level and had to avoid coverage, which could have been the goal. As mentioned, the same reform aim to enhance the quality of medical care and finally moderating the growth regarding costs. The Act intends to classify goals of reform as *latent goals*. The policy classifies three primary goals stated in the definition, as well as an overview of the policy, as *manifest goals* and whose main agenda is to make the life of those from the lower income households better. Almost 5 years later since its inception, some of the social effects are notable and therefore this section tends to list and analyses some of the social effects. Understanding the problem, however, is the crucial factor as it is the primary objective of this section, as well as the only item that can be used to conclude.

Some of the foreseen impacts of the Act was the hope to improve the overall well-being, as well as the income of the Americans especially those in the fifth bottom level of the income distribution. Most Americans had insurance and would not be affected by the reforms. At the same time, some projections included that those who would receive or have access to subsidized insurance would realize income gain, which might be higher. Five years into the implementation and the impact or results started showing. The results are a clear indication of the number of uninsured people reduced but not as projected by the U.S. Congressional Budget Office (CBO) who gave the following sizes of those affected by the problem the Act addressing. The scope that still affected the question is as follows:

- Number of uninsured individuals since 2010 estimated to be 15 million.

- 35 million people are estimated to still require insurance.

- 12 million more people enrolled into Medicare since 2010.

- The number of those receiving subsidiaries for coverage regarding exchange is 7.7 million.

- The size of the individuals who have insurances through a federal trade or the state is estimated at 11 million.

A survey conducted by Carman (2014) involving American Physicians provided various responses linked to grading ACA as a vehicle for the health care reforms, as well as addressing the underlying problem. According to the results obtained, 3.7% of those who took part in the study gave the law an A, while 21.7% gave an overall grade of B. Further, 28.8% graded C, and the majority, while 21.1% and 24.7% ranked a D, as well as a grade of E respectively (Carman, 2014). From the results gathered, it is a clear indication that the reforms do not address the problem that many people remain affected by the issues related to health care. Regarding the affordability of the necessary insurance, the most affected are those from the low-income levels. Despite the impact of these reforms not only affecting the financial well-being of lower-income families, but they also have the capability of changing other social values such as marriages or union formations, and fertility, as well as divorce. These factors are the dominant social values related to the problem because they have the capability of creating conflicts.

Some critics of ACA speculated that ACA could lead to unintended impact: increased rate of divorce (Ewing, 2015). Ewing (2015) argued that many American couples' decision to stay together is driven by the simple reason that they may not afford health insurance when living on their own. The argument was that from the family law perspective, the successful implementation of ACA could eliminate barriers to divorce especially for affected couples. As a consequent, there could be increased rate of divorce. In line with this argument, Ewing argued that ACA could potentially impact on spousal maintenance claims; impact on women; encourage divorce among the middle and lower-income couples; change the negotiations about division of community property among couples; and benefit the previously dependent spouse. Ewing further advanced that the implimentation of ACA could influence individuals who initially stayed in unhappy marriages to quit because they do not need to maintain their insurance coverage. The increase in the devorce rates seems not to have happened as the view by Ewing and others seem unsupported by research findings by Slusky and Ginther (2017). In this study, Slusky and Ginther used ACA's Medicaid expansion which enabled couples to qualify for Medicaid, to create a model of medical divorce. The model predicts divorce settlements are maximum when the joint assets of couple exceeds the exempted asset level. Slusky and Ginther used Medicaid as an exogenous variable predicting incidence of divorce among Americans.

Slusky and Ginther (2017) found that ACA lowers the medical divorce rates rather than increases in the divorce rate as was envisioned. In particular, Slusky and Ginther noted that ACA's expansion reduces by 11.6% the prevalence of divorce among Americans aged 50-64. The reduction in the prevalence of divorce among the elderly Americans appears to be supported by several stories of individuals who, before the implementation of ACA, opted for divorce with a view to qualify for Medicaid and therefore save their retirement savings. For these individuals, the asset test made it difficult for their spouses with costly long-term diseases such as dementia or cancer to qualify for Medicaid to retain the majority of their retirement savings. Examples of these stories include a story by Nicholas Kristof of the New York Times; and a story by Goldman (2008). In the first story, Kristof (2009) narrated a story about a lady whose spouse was diagnosed with dementia. The lady faced a situation in which their entire retirement savings could be drained because as a result of spending towards caring for the ailing husband. The lady opted to legally divorse her spouse to shield and save her assets. The husband eventually drew down his assets and became poor and eventually qualified for Medicaid. By opting for divorce, the lady saved her retirement benefits.

In a similar story, Goldman (2008) narrated a story of a spouse in Indiana in which a woman diagnosed with cancer divorced her husband, a decision that enabled her to qualify for Medicaid and paid for her cancer treatment. A study by Chen (2013) researched eligibility to Medicare (at age 65) showing increases in the divorce rates especially in states without non-expanded Medicaid. ACA to some extent impacted the prevalence of divorce at least in a positive way rather than in a negative way as envisaged. The Act ostensibly fixed the underlying issue that prompted divorce especially among Americans aged 50-64 by expanding Medicaid to cover all Americans under 65 whose incomes lies below the 138% of the U.S. federal poverty line, regardless of the amount of assets one owns (Sung, Skopec, & Wadmann, 2015). Prior to the implementation of ACA, many American States imposed stringent asset requirements. However, it is worth noting that reprieve only happened in states that implemented Medicaid expansion. Couples in Medicaid non-expansion states would still face the dilemma of divorce on the basis of medical conditions.

Economic Analysis

The U.S. government spends about one fifth of its gross domestic product (GDP) on the health care sector (Catlin & Cowan, 2015). As revealed by Catlin and Cowan (2015), the U.S. health care expenditure steadily increased from 5% of the GDP in 1960 to 17.4% in 2013. Catlin and Cowan identified private and public initiatives, prices, recessions, legislation and policy changes are key factors that influence the spending by the U.S. government of health care sector. A suggestion is that reforms such as those suggested by ACA have implications on the economy of the entire nation. Research by Price and Saltzman (2013) indicated the positive economic effects of ACA would be modest since federal dollars flow from one state to another with a lower per capita income. The funding of the law, however, may be at the regional level with a ripple effect on the economy; the ripple effect known as multipliers. The funding process means that the additional funds that the hospitals, as well as the doctors, will have access to will be used for various functions such as buying medical equipment and paying the salaries of their employees. The employees will, therefore, have the income to purchase services and goods from different business around their areas of residence. As a result, the initial injection of the funds circulates with the entire economy. To understand how funds flow through the U.S. economy and multiply, the figure below is vital for illustrations (see Figure 1), it is essential to understand the economic effects associated with the reforms about financing have the same reverberations.

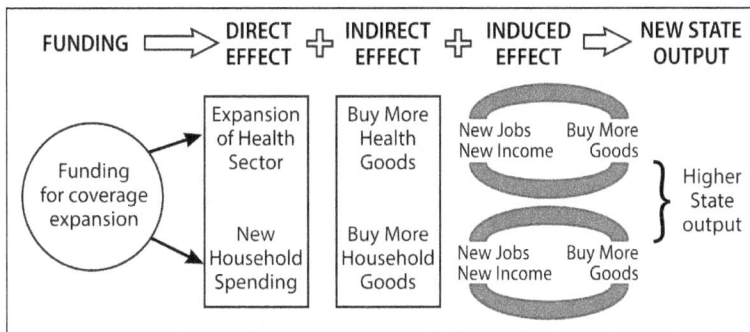

Funding ACA (Figure 1)

When conducting economic analysis, it is crucial to take into consideration factors such the functioning of the economy as one entity, inflation because of the policy, income, and address resultant unemployment problems. The mentioned problems will be referred as the macroeconomic analysis of ACA. By contrast, the microeconomic analysis conducted on this section highlights the potential effects of ACA on the behavior of individuals, markets-motivation to work, firms, the supply of commodities and finally the cost of rent. The Act signifies a crucial transfer of assets to low and middle-income families in a simplified way of subsidized health insurance. Theoretically, the transfer of these resources as stipulated by the reforms should be able to increase the targeted individuals, while at the same time reducing any form of financial risk that may head their way, especially those associated with high costs of medical bills.

When the law took effect in 2013, almost 2 million people already selected a health insurance plan in the marketplace, and another 80% were likely to choose their plan as well (Borelli, Bujanda, & Maier, 2016). The provisions of the law increased the speed with which the people from said class acquired affordable health care service and in turn enabled them meet some of the other pressing needs. The urgent requirements achieved have in turn increased the demand for goods and services throughout the economy (Graves & Swartz, 2017). The increasing demand is an inordinate sign for future needs. It is important to note that despite the reforms being executed the unemployment rate remains elevated, but projections include the ability to reduce as the changes take effect. The changes have the capability of creating jobs for the unemployed to make it easier for those seeking employment to have access without struggle. ACA has a significant effect on the labor market by defining or affecting labor supply and demand.

The reforms encouraged self-employment and entrepreneurship for those unable to find jobs while at the same time subjected the larger firms to penalties if they fail to provide affordable coverage to all their employees. These employees are those who work more than 30 hours a week, and therefore it is true that the reforms mostly affect the economy despite that the changes may be minute. In turn, the threats that come with the law changed the behaviors of individuals, as well as firms requiring everyone to have insurances as those who failed to comply with the Act were subject to fines. In doing so, ACA reduces the long-term country deficits and lays the foundation required for future growth. For example, a study by Benjamin Tal (2012) claimed the USCBO estimated the reforms to ACA will have reduced the current deficit by at least $109 between 2013 through to 2022 fiscal year. After this time the same the same what? projects a reduction of the same deficit by 0.5% of the GDP in the subsequent years. Over a 10-year period, the USCBO estimates the gap reduces by $1.6 trillion (Tal, 2012). The reduction is a significant impact on the entire economy. The same projection will reduce any chances of inflation, increase income, reduce unemployment, and bring about growth in the economy.

Since its enactment, the law impacted both the patients and

hospitals, enabling most of them to have adequate equipment to help people get better treatment. At the same time, those who could not afford insurance can now access health care services, reducing the cost incurred in case they did not have insurance. Opportunity costs are a significant factor when conducting economic analysis as they form the basis, or any economic model developed for research. For this case, opportunity cost comes to play because the labor market is already cost effective and that the system or the economy can incorporate more workers who in turn help the economy.

Political Analysis

Politically, ACA faced opposition from different quotas and at different levels: at the proposal level, enactment level, and the implementation level.

At the proposal level, the reformers of the health care reform sought to design a bill that could meet central meet policy goals of reforming health care without major disruption to the health care system that was in existence. These reformers understood that the reforms had to meet appeal to two audience's else opposition could arise. The audiences were the public and the health care industry. These reformers targeted the health care industry audience with a view to avoid the opposition from the major health care industry players. Industry players eliminated previous efforts aimed at reforming the health care insurance using industry-financed opposition. The reformers targeted the public using reforms aimed at addressing people's biggest worries, while avoiding the alteration of the financial arrangements that offered health care insurance coverage to 85% of Americans.

Two groups designed the approach to national reform in Massachusetts in 2006. The Massachusetts advocates, who included doctors, labor unions, hospitals, and health care consumers made the decision to focus on covering all the residents of the state, rather than focus on controlling costs. Health care reformers borrowed from liberal and conservative ideas and came up with an approach that appealed to large Democratic majority and the Republican Governor Mitt Romney. Reformers developed a framework built that became law. A framework built on four pillars of the health care coverage system embraced by President Obama: Medicare, Medicaid, individually purchased insurance, and the employer provided coverage. The state-imposed fines that encouraged employers in Massachusetts to continue offering health care coverage. The state increased the U.S. federal child health insurance program and the Medicaid eligibility limit to cover children and adults above the poverty line. However, the state left the Medicare program untouched. These were liberal ideas that resonated to those of insurers and health care provides without making any disruption to payment arrangements.

The conservative group, Heritage Foundation (1973) (as cited in Roy, 2012), created an innovation in the individual market that blended the liberal and conservative policies. The innovation idea raised by requiring individuals to purchase health insurance. The idea aimed at making insurance coverage to most people from the health insurance marketplace. Reformers made the idea appealing to liberals by regulating the new market and offering individuals income-based subsidies to purchase the insurance coverage. The regulations included continuing insurance reforms that already existed in Massachusetts, including charging individuals a higher premium for their medical history and bans on denying people coverage because of a preexisting condition, limiting entry to coverage plans that met cost and quality standard, and establishing set benefit. The major constituencies found the Massachusetts' framework appealing. The framework appealed to consumer groups by making the making affordable coverage affordable and accessible to individuals. Details of the Act seemingly assured health insurers new customers. Owners of hospitals anticipated more patients and most of the patients would be insured. From the perspective of the public, the coverage would be an affordable and positive change.

It was only advocators of the single-payer or public health insurance who were not embraced by the Massachusetts framework. For these advocators of the single-payer, the single-pager approach was better to the Massachusetts' policy because public health insurance meant that one government-run insurance plan insured everyone. The single-payer proponents framed the public health insurance as one that extends Medicare for all. The proponents of single-payer model saw the single-payer as the best approach to implement at the national level. These advocates of the single-pager framework constituted a significant number in the movement that advocated for the health reform. The support deemed crucial to successful winning comprehensive health reforms nationally.

However, divisions existed in the health reform movement for decades on how to work with the multiplier U.S. health care system and how to implement reforms based on the U.S. national health insurance. The division made it difficult for the health reformation movement to mount a unified campaign that would support reforms and work to overcome opposition to actual legislation. In addition, there were deep political flaws in the single-payer policy. The single-payer worked against 150 million individuals with employer-based coverage. The adoption of the single-pager framework meant Americans with employer-based coverage would lose the government insurance. The policy reflected a proposal by Kirsch (2003) and another model by Hacker and the Economic & Social Research Institute (Hacker, 2001).

Policy makers introduced another policy innovation (i.e., the public option in 2009 to help bridge the gap among the advocators of the health reforms and appeal to the public). Policy makers considered the public option a bridge between the two competing health reform visions. The public option intended to provide a choice of public health insurance plans that competes with the regulated private insurance plan. The proposal appealed to many progressive health reform movements. However, the proposal faced opposition from the health insurance industry and the conservatives. The mainstream health care providers, including drug companies, hospital, and doctors did not favor the public option. Finally, health care providers, the health insurers, the Obama Administration, and the Democrats in the U.S. Congress agreed and accepted the Massachusetts' approach. The supporters of Massachusetts' framework saw the approach as offering new customers financing mechanisms already in existence. Insurance firms were ready and willing to offer insurance coverage to Americans with preexisting conditions. However, the insurance company had one condition: the requirement to purchase health insurance coverage would prevent the problem of Americans from remaining without an insurance coverage until they needed medical care. The Obama administration and the Democrats focused on seeking support from the health industry toward the reform, including a multi-stakeholder process by the Senate Health, Education Pensions, and Labor Committee under Senator Ted Kennedy and conversations that came before the election of Obama.

The Chairman of the Senate Finance Committee, Max Baucus, and the White House negotiated industry specific trade-offs with the key health care industry players. The negotiation secured the support of health care industry players who agreed to the deal to have changes made in some health care payments on condition that there would be more Americans insured as new customers and there would be no other reduction in their health care revenues.

The Democrats struck a deal with the American Prescription Drug lobbying group (PhRMA). In the deal, Democrats agreed to reverse two long-held positions of opposing the importation of medicine from Canada and to negotiate drug prices in Medicare.

On its part, PhRMA agreed to support the health care legislation by financing advertisements and reducing the prices charged on drugs in the Medicare prescription plan for seniors (Hacker, 2001). Democrats secured the support of the American Hospital Association and the American Medical Association (AMA) for ACA legislation achieved through negotiations.

The Obama administration understood that the Clinton administration spent much of the time developing its own bill. The which one? administration decided to minimize possible opposition to ACA legislation by the members of the U.S. Congress by working with the Democrats in the U.S. Congress. The White House avoided possible delays to the legislation by the members of Congress by avoiding fanning intramural fights. Democrats in both houses agreed to write readily reconcilable bills. The next effort made by the Obama administration to get the legislation through was fielding a well-organized and funded national and grassroots campaign to demonstrate to members of the U.S. Congress that the bill had grassroots support.

Starting in 2007, several progressive organizations, including community organizing networks, constituency groups, think tanks, netroots, constituency groups, and unions prepared for a Democrat winning the presidency and the passage of the ACA bill. Health care for America (HCAN) ran several grassroots field campaigns in 40 states alongside press conferences in 38 states and 43 cities across America (Armstrong, 2010). In addition, HCAN spent $50 million on national TV ads to respond to conservative opponents' anti-government rhetoric (Armstrong, 2010). The effort by HCAN bolstered Democratic support in the U.S. Congress. The effort prevailed on conservative Democrats to support the bill (Armstrong, 2010). Other major groups, including labor unions, ran grassroots campaigns for netroots. Netroots are networks of bloggers who usually form on the internet to initiate grassroots support for a political cause. President Obama pushed hard, moved fast, and kept moving after his presidential victory. The President conducted a health care summit with major health care stakeholders and congressional leaders in March of 2009 and actual legislation started to move by June of 2009. The president received assistance from Senate Majority leader Harry Reid and House Speaker Nancy Pelosi.

At the enactment of the ACA Bill and its signing into law by President Obama, ACA faced some opposition especially from the Republicans. As indicated by Rigby, Clark, and Pelika (2014), party politics played out during the enactment of Obamacare. Rigby et al. also revealed that passing ACA took place without Republican votes. Passage of the Act was accompanied by intense criticism from the Republicans that the majority party *rammed through* the legislative process.

On the contrary, many Democrats emphasized that the passage of the ACA bill was necessary to conclude the extensive debate over health care reform in the United States. As noted by Rigby et al. (2014), the Democrats passed the bill on grounds that the bill was necessary to bring important reforms in the U.S. health care system. Worth noting is that the intention of ACA itself is an improvement of the previous amendments made to the Health Care Act with the purpose of making health care services available to all Americans.

There are several differences between Obamacare and the old Health Care Act (Borelli, Bujanda, & Maier, 2016). For example, Obamacare requires coverage for all pre-existing conditions, while the old healthcare system did not require insurers coverage of all the pre-existing conditions. Obamacare utilizes the payer's premium (i.e., free), the old healthcare system used a co-pay meaning that included was a deductible fee in addition to the required premium. Obamacare requires insurers to allow children to remain on their parents' insurance coverage plan until age 26, while the old system allowed insurers to eliminate children from their parents' health insurance plan upon reaching age 21.

Obamacare includes contraception under preventative care, while the old system does not include contraception. Obamacare requires individuals to purchase health insurance for themselves, as well as for their dependents and imposes a penalty for those who fail to do so at the time of filing their taxes. The old health care health program did not include this provision. Last, Obamacare made it mandatory for organizations with 50+ employees to offer healthcare insurance coverage to more than 95% of their employees and the coverage to be affordable and offer minimum value. The old health care program did not impose such requirements to employers (Borelli et al., 2016). Obamacare is a regulatory overhaul of the U.S. healthcare system. ACA subsidies and insurance exchange institute mandates aimed at increasing the scope, affordability, and quality of healthcare within the U.S. mixed market system. The reforms, as well as the program, worked better than anticipated in most respects. Each day, the number of the uninsured individuals dropped, despite Republicans controlling most states. Republicans are not supporters of the Act and are opposed to the reforms. It is surprising that 17 states, specifically under the Republican governors, refused to expand the Medicaid program as required by law. These states that refused to expand the Medicaid program as of 2014 included Alabama, Florida, Georgia, Kansas, Mississippi, Missouri, Nebraska, North Carolina, Oklahoma, South Carolina, South Dakota, Tennessee, Uttar, Wisconsin, and Wyoming (Kaiser Family Foundation [KFF], 2018).

CHAPTER 6

ACA: Myths versus Facts

Owing to the abundant revisions and the length of ACA, the law presented many misunderstandings and condemnation. Myths about the law continued to rise with lawsuits debating ACA's legitimacy, significantly muddling already-confused Americans. Similar to most politically discordant subjects, when considering ACA, one might find difficulty in separating facts from myths. Therefore, it is important to revisit some of the misconceptions about the law as demonstrated herein.

Myth 1: ACA is responsible for the rising health insurance costs.

Fact: Health insurance premiums, especially the company-sponsored family health insurance premiums, increased since 2005. As revealed by the Kaiser Family Foundation Survey (KFF, 2013b), health insurance premiums for privately-purchased plans rose by 18% between 2005 and 2010. There was a 39% increase in health insurance premiums following the opening of the health insurance exchanges in 2013. However, as revealed by Kaiser Family Foundation Survey, 46% of individuals who enrolled for the health insurance program experienced lower premiums. The drop-in premium demonstrates that health insurance costs increased prior to the enactment of ACA. More revealing is that since the enactment of ACA, health insurance premiums increased at a slower rate (i.e., 3.8% compared to 4.8%), suggesting that ACA is not to blame for the rising health insurance costs.

MYTH 2: ACA forces people to pay higher health insurance premium for services they do not need, such as maternity care, childbirth, and pregnancy.

Fact: In all health insurance plans, individuals pay for services they may never need. For example, women may never need to test for prostate cancer and a marathon runner may never need diabetes care. The childbirth coverage under ACA intends to lower the overall health care costs. Medicaid covers 50% of all childbirth. ACA helps reduce the cost of women's prenatal care, ensuring that it is less expensive than the cost of emergency room treatment

MYTH 3: ACA is socialized medicine, like the United Kingdom (UK) or in Canada.

Fact: The truth is that ACA deviates from the UK and Canadian socialized medicine. The Act reduced socialized medicine costs. In the UK, the government pays most medical costs of doctors, while in the U.S., the federal government employs doctors. The Canadian system is like America's Medicaid and Medicare. ACA expands Medicaid to middle-income families

MYTH 4: ACA allows government bureaucrats rather than the doctor to decide the treatment for individuals. ACA intrudes into the patient-doctor relationship.

Fact: ACA does not impact the doctor-patient relationship. The doctors make the decisions regarding medical treatment and insurance companies make the decisions regarding coverage. The insurance company makes the decision regarding how much the company pays the doctor and how much policies would cover. ACA did not change the Medicare and Medicare system.

MYTH 5: ACA cuts benefits for Americans on Medicare.

Fact: Medicare benefits were not cut following the enactment of

ACA. However, ACA reduced funding for Medicare by $716 million? Says who? . The reduction in Medicare funding affected providers rather than recipients in the following ways:

- ACA changed the way hospitals were paid. It changed from the *fee-for-service* payment for every procedure and test to value-based care. The new system allowed individuals to receive better care from hospitals at a relatively lower cost.

- The enactment of ACA led to the reduction in the amount received by Medicare Advantage insurance providers. It restricted increase in costs to 1% above the economic growth rate.

- ACA increased Medicare benefits, including free preventative care such as mammograms and physicals, an annual wellness visit, and the closing of the donut hole in the prescription drug benefit.

MYTH 6: ACA allows the government to take-over health care.

Fact: Under ACA, the private insurance market still exists with more people eligible for coverage. ACA serves to end discriminatory practices that for many years prevented millions of Americans from keeping or getting insurance coverage by holding insurance companies accountable.

MYTH 7: ACA is largely aimed at increasing taxes.

Fact: ACA may be considered tax relief to millions of Americans. It allows millions of Americans to be covered by insurance. Americans will no longer be required to pay the extra costs built into their premiums to cover for costs incurred by individuals without insurance.

MYTH 8: ACA makes the insurance coverage of health care less secure.

Fact: ACA makes the insurance coverage of health care more secure. It does not deny families insurance coverage because of a pre-existing condition. It provides that insurance plan used by millions of Americans is also used by the members of the U.S. Congress.

MYTH 9: ACA penalizes small employees.

Fact: ACA gives small businesses tax credits to enable them to purchase insurance and allows them to band together to obtain lower rates like big corporations. The tax credit makes insurance coverage for small business affordable.

To summarize, numerous revisions of ACA exists. The law lost a basic understanding throughout the development of the number of revisions. The theory of ACA caused public fears and citizens drew to their own conclusions. With little clarity available, this book details and clears up some of the myths. The legitimacy of the ACA still fuels debate across political groups in America. The goal of the author continues to be providing clarity to small businesses to avoid harmful belief of ACA myths.

CHAPTER 7

Implications of ACA on Public Health Policy and Practice

The Affordable Care Act deserves the acknowledgment as a seminal moment in the public health policy in the United States. The Act established the previously absent legal health protections, guaranteeing accessibility to reasonable health insurance coverage from birth through retirement. ACA was envisaged that after full implementation, the number of uninsured Americans would reduce by more than half. The reduction did not happen. More than 50% of Americans remain uninsured. ACA has distinct major objectives characterized by 10 discrete jurisdictive titles. The objectives include:

- To achieve widespread coverage that is more than 50% via joint responsibility among the people, government, and companies. Joint responsibility is the major and foremost aim.

- To reduce costs and enable more Americans to access health insurance. ACA does this by providing Americans with subsidies in form of premium tax credits. The subsidy serves to reduce costs for low income households.

- To support innovative medical care delivery methods aimed at lowering costs of health care.

In general, the many provisions advocated for by the public health community were contained in the final bill signed into ACA by President Obama. ACA has several sections that included the public health component. One such section is the Prevention of Chronic Diseases & Improvement Public Health clause. ACA addresses goals of public health in three ways: (a) ACA increases access to health care related preventive services; (b) offered new incentives for wellness and prevention programs; and (c) established new structures and programs that focused on enhanced funding for health care programs. ACA also focuses on meeting public health objectives (Chait & Glied, 2018).

Expansion of Public Capacity

ACA created a comprehensive public health strategy encompassing the Prevention & Public Health Fund; the National Prevention; Public Health Council; and Health Promotion Program. ACA dedicated $15 billion to the Prevention and Public Health Fund (Haberkorn, 2012; Rigby, 2011). The Fund and the Public Health Council was aimed at increasing the public health capacity to facilitate the Centres for Disease Control & Prevention (CDC) establish national timely public health programs (Etheridge, 1992). The Prevention Fund was designed for the CDC to facilitate it its objective of pursuing specific and targeted national initiatives such as National Diabetes Prevention program and Smokers campaign (McAfee, Davis, Alexander, Pechacek, & Bunnell, 2013). The Council consists of Cabinet-level representatives from different agencies with the Surgeon General as its chair. Since 2010, the Council reported success in its undertakings. For example, in 2011, the Council released the National Prevention Strategy that articulated for the health priorities at the national level throughout the United States. The Council achieved significant success in the four pillars advocated for by the public health community: providing preventive services in the community and clinical settings; creating healthy communities; helping consumer make informed health decisions and eliminating health disparities (Chait & Glied, 2018).

The Council achieved significant success in priority areas that were advocated for by the public health community. These priority areas included increasing healthy eating; reducing substance use; emotional and mental well-being and violent-and injury-free living (Rojas et al., 2016). In addition, the Council successfully encouraged the Department of Health & Human Services (HHS) and other departments and agencies to consider public health issues when establishing health policies (Navarro, 2016). A typical example was the 2016 ban on smoking in public housing by a member of the Council (i.e., Department of Housing & Urban Development (HUD) (Centers for Disease Control and Prevention [CDC], 2014; Navarro, 2016).

Other aspects of ACA successfully expanded public health capacity. ACA allocated funding used for improving public health laboratory capacity. Funds were distributed in six largest municipal health departments; eight U.S. territories; and 50 state health departments (CDC, 2018). ACA reauthorized the National Health Service Corps (NHSC) and increased funds for health practitioners and public health fellowships (Lau, Adams, Park, Boscardin, & Irwin, 2014; Williams & Redhead, 2010). Furthermore, ACA provided $9.5 billion for patient e-services and operations, and $1.5 billion for renovation and construction, as well as funding for nurse-managed health clinics and school-based health centres. These funding strengthened community health centres throughout the United States (Williams & Redhead, 2010). An additional 6,000 clinicians were trained because of the expansion of NHSC. The trained clinicians provided primary care to about 10 million people across the United States (KFF, 2013a). Again, by providing new funding to health centres at the federal level, ACA facilitated health centres to serve 3.7 million existing and new patients (KFF, 2013a). The Act increased funding to facilitate clinicians practicing in underserved primary care areas, as well as funding for loan repayment programmed for these health care.

ACA created the Center for Medicare & Medicaid Innovation (CMMI) within the Centre for Medicare & Medicaid Services (CMS), which created new opportunities for funding of the prevention programs (Chait & Glied, 2018). One CMMI-initiative provided an avenue for millions of dollars to be channeled through the federal government to the states. These funds facilitated states to use health care system resources to improve their population health and health care systems (Rojas et al., 2016). As noted by Rojas et al. (2016), by 2017, the CMMI-initiated State Innovation Model (SIM) Program funded efforts in Washington, DC, three territories, and 34 states, to improve the delivery of health care and population health, while decreasing costs (Rojas et al., 2016). The CMMI-initiated program also enabled states to receive funding to implement and create state health improvement plans and plans to integrate community-based, public health and behavioural health services (RTI Int, 2016). These plans are targeted at preventative drivers of poor health in various states (RTI Int., 2016). As of 2016, 30 states received funding used for designing the health model with 15 states with model design funding receiving grants for testing their models (Chait & Glied, 2018). These funded states created plans for new and improved health care workforce models and created accountable care organizations that establish linkages between these models and social services, community organizations and public health (RTI Int., 2016). States such as Oregon, Minnesota, and Maine created Accountable Communities for Health using SIM funding (Hall, Fendrick, Zochowski, & Dalton, 2014). These accountable Communities for Health focuses on integrating nonmedical and medical services and on population prevention to increase population health and greater healthy equity (Hallet al., 2014).

A report by Sobel, Salganicoff, Kurani, and Wiens (2015) on SIM states revealed positive result. The report showed that 50% of the SIM states were halfway in achieving the goal of using value-based delivery models to provide 80% of health care (Sobel, Salganicoff, Kurani, & Wiens, 2015). However, some SIM states faced challenges in integrating public health into the SIM initiatives (Sobel et al., 2015). Furthermore, many of SIM states do not have comprehensive data systems that can be used by state agencies to monitor the effect of the new changes and new programs (Sobel et al., 2015).

Increasing Clinical Coverage

ACA required all insurers to offer preventative services by expanding to health care insurance coverage that include preventative services without cost-sharing. ACA led to expansion of preventive care (Chait & Glied, 2018).

The Act required that insurance companies to provide free coverage of preventative to patients. The requirement provided 71 million Americans with free primary car, cancer screening, and access to vaccines among other services (Skopec & Sommers, 2013). However, the impact of the free preventative care on health outcome is unclear. Studies reported mixed results regarding the impact of free covered preventative services to patients since the passage of ACA. However, the extension of preventative services without cost-sharing to individuals with private insurance resulted in increased cholesterol checks, blood pressure, and flu vaccinations (Han, Yabroff, Guy Zheng, & Jemal 2015). However, there was no change in breast, colorectal, and cervical cancer screenings (Han et al., 2015). Similarly, ACA has a provision aimed at doing away with the Medicare's no-cost preventing services cost-sharing from Medicare. Studies found mixed result regarding the impact of using these services (Chung et al., 2015; Hamman & Kapinos, 2015).

Prior to the implementation of ACA, many beneficiaries of Medicare accessed no-cost sharing preventive services via supplemented insurance plans. The mixed results reported by Chung et al. (2015) and Hamman and Kapinos, (2015) regarding the effect of using these services may explain why this change in the requirement of these services had limited beneficiaries of Medicare. On the contrary, studies on individuals who gained health insurance coverage via the expansion reported improvement in terms of the use of these services (Simon, Soni, & Cawley, 2017; Sommers, Blendon, Orav, & Epstein, 2016). These studies reported increases in HIV screening; diabetes screening; and preventive visits among individuals with newly safeguarded Medicaid. In addition, these studies reported an increase in the proportion of Americans with excellent health and a decrease in the use of department use among these newly ensured Medicaid individuals (Simon et al., 2017; Sommers et al., 2016). Sabik and Adunlin (2017) reviewed studies that examined the impact of ACA on screening of cancer and found that early detection of cancer and the use of screenings increased among the vulnerable populations, including new Medicaid enrolees, and Medicare enrolees previously without free coverage. In another study that investigated the impact of expansion of employer-sponsored health insurance coverage to young adult dependents aged under 26 as provided for in ACA, found a 3-5% expansion in coverage of young adults who received preventive services (Lau, Adams, Park, Boscardin, & Irwin, 2014).

ACA included contraception as a preventive service in women, which substantially changed the payments for these contraception services (Navarro, 2016). For example, Navarro (2016) reported 50% increase in the proportion of claims without cost sharing for contraception services notably intrauterine devices (IUDs) following the implantations of ACA. Similarly, Sonfield, Tapales, Jones, and Finer (2015) observed an increase in the use of the ring, injectable contraception, and the pill following the implementation of ACA. However, there are no empirical studies that demonstrated that the inclusion of birth control programs as a preventive service, without cost-sharing, can lead to increased use of costly IUDs or other birth control measures. There was a significant increase in the IUD use in 2013, after the implementation of the ACA coverage provision on birth control. However, the increased use of IUD remained consistent with the previous increased use of IUD (Navarro, 2016).

The low awareness among women of the ACA coverage provisions and the insurance companies' non-compliance with the provision may contribute to the low use of contraceptive implants and IUDs. The nationally representative survey revealed that the 65% of women were not informed about ACA's contraceptive coverage (Chuang et al., 2015). In another survey by Hall, Fendrick, Zochowski, and Dalton (2014), it was reported that 11% of the Pennsylvania women were informed about the ACA IUD coverage. The survey suggests that as women learn about the benefit of ACA contraceptive coverage, the insurance companies increase compliance with ACA IUD coverage. The increased compliance could expand the proportion of women embracing long-acting reversible contraceptives and IUDs.

Incentivizing Wellness and Performance

Another ACA's public health initiative encompasses incentives to patients, employers, states, and providers to improve health. The Act increased the ceiling on incentives targeted at workplace wellness from 20% to 30% of the health care costs. The Act permitted employers to increase by 50% of health insurance premiums for participating in smoking cessation programs (Madison, Schmidt, & Volpp, 2013). In addition, the Act made available grant funds for the creation of workplace wellness programs by small businesses. ACA mandated CDC to evaluate existing wellness initiatives and existing federal health initiatives (Koh & Sebelius, 2010).

One of the incentive-based programs provided in ACA is the Medicaid Incentives for Prevention of Chronic Diseases (MIPCD).

Ten states could test the use of incentive-based prevention program for demonstration purposes (RTI Int., 2016). However, there is no evidence demonstrating the success of these incentive-based programs as a tool for improving public health. There are, however, studies that show that Medicaid expansion could improve public health even without incentive-based prevention program (Maclean, Pesko, & Hill, 2017). For example, Maclean, Pesko, and Hill (2017) found that states with expanded Medicaid reported 36% increase in the prescription for smoking cessation medication compared to states with non-expanded Medicaid. These medications reported an increase of 28% in Medicaid payments (Maclean et al., 2017). Results of this study suggested that expanding even without additional interventions, expanding Medicaid coverage can lead to increased attempts to quit smoking.

During the debating and drafting of ACA, public health experts suggested that the health care reform should be aimed at extending health insurance coverage as well as encompass population health. These experts suggested that funding should be dedicated towards ACA and policy attention were given to the legislation to facilitate the improvement in population health (Bassett, 2009; Chernichovsky & Leibowitz, 2010; Farley, 2009; Goodman, 2009; Wallace & Sommers, 2015). Advocates of public health suggested that health reform could be used to address other issues beyond medical care, such as social determinants of health, including objectives such as improving access to vegetables and fruits in schools and reducing food insecurity in the United States (Bassett, 2009; Skopec & Sommers, 2013). Public health advocates called on the health reformers to consider creating community health worker corps and community-based prevention (Bassett, 2009; Goodman, 2009).

These public health community suggested that there is need to increase the percentage of health spending directed towards public health and suggested that the health reform should consider promoting the use of enhanced regulatory tools to improve nutrition, encourage exercise, and reduce smoking (Bassett, 2009; Farley, 2009). These advocators of public health also suggested that the health reform legislation should emphasize structural changes, notably the reorganizational of the U.S. public health departments to focus on chronic disease and the environment (Farley, 2009). These public health advocators pushed for the legislation to increase funding the prevention of the population-level chronic disease, as well as the bolstering of the enrolment outreach for insurance programs reflected the prevention components, including the Children's Health Insurance Program (CHIP) and Medicaid (Skopec & Sommers, 2013).

Overall, ACA increased the number of Americans with health insurance coverage by 9.3 million Americans between 2013 and 2014 (Carman, 2014). However, the expansion of health care insurance coverage by ACA has had an unanticipated impact on the America's health care system, particularly the impact on the clinical care services country offers, including family planning, child and maternal health, infectious disease control, cancer care, and other specific services (Buck, 2011; Koh, & Sebelius, 2010). Studies on ACA demonstrated that the Act successfully accomplished the objectives of improving Americans' access to medical care and reducing the America's insurance rate (Altman, 2016; Avery, Finegold, & Whitman, 2016; KFF, 2016; Shartzer, Long, & Anderson, 2015; Skopec, Waidmann, Sung, & Dean, 2016). For example, studies revealed that by 2016, substantial improvements had been noted in terms of measure of access to health care and the percentage of the Americans without health insurance coverage was at the lowest level ever noted (Blumenthal, Abrams, & Nuzum, 2015). In general, the broad goal of promoting these efforts by the public health community was to make certain ACA focuses on improving health and eliminate health disparities across communities.

CHAPTER 8

2017 Market Views on Small Business Health Insurance

There are a number of provisions associated with ACA that restructure the health insurance market. The reforms aim at putting American beneficiaries back in charge of their health insurance and their health care. Moreover, the purpose of the reforms is to make sure that Americans receive value for their premiums. The law provided a level playing field after taking stern measures against irrational health coverage premiums and holding insurance companies responsible for unwarranted premium increases. ACA impacts small businesses that have multiple entities under joint ownership. Notably, the rule applies to companies that work together to offer services to third parties.

The mandate proclaims that when the total number of workers in the collective organized or allied service group is beyond 50, then the group is an Applicable Large Employer. ACA establishes that Small businesses provide health insurance to its workers by offering them tax credit. The tax credit is 50% of the employer-paid premiums and 35% for tax-exempt employers. The legislation allows small employers to claim tax credit for a maximum of two consecutive taxable years. The terms of the law provides that small businesses can claim tax credit by purchasing a Qualified Health Plan under the Small Business Health Options Program Marketplace. ACA discourages the avoidance by Small businesses to purchase health plan for their employers by imposing a penalty for those that fail to comply. The argument is that failure to purchase a health plan for an employer is substandard to market reforms and would subject the employer to a penalty of up to $36,500 per year per affected employee. According to the rule, the employer arrangement that pays or reimburses individual health premiums for employees defines a group health insurance plan. The group plan is subject to a penalty of $100 per employee perday. Meaning that ACA bars small businesses from paying directly the health costs of employees or helping employees with health costs. ACA also provides:

- **Annual Limits:** Starting in 2014, the law banned annual dollar limits. Plans could no longer have annual dollar limits on essential benefits coverage, such as physician, hospital, and / or pharmacy benefits.

- **Young Adults Coverage:** According to the law, if a plan covered a child, a parent can insure their children on their health coverage plan until the age of 26.

- **Market Rating Reforms:** These are necessities that standardize the way health insurance providers can price products, introduce a different level of transparency, and the impartiality of the pricing of premiums.

- **Medical Loss Ratio:** Medical Loss Ratio (MLR) is the fraction of premium revenues used on clinical services and quality enhancement. The law demands that health insurers provide data on MLR and produce rebates to enrollees if the percentage is below the minimum standards.

- **The Mental Health Parity and Addiction Equity Act (MHPAEA):** A federal law that typically averts health insurance providers and group health plans that deliver substance use disorder and mental health profits from daunting less satisfactory benefit limitations on those benefits than on surgical / medical profits.

- **Minimum Essential Coverage (MEC):** The MEC is the coverage level necessary for an individual to meet the personal responsibility requirement under ACA. Included in the coverage are individual market policies, job-based coverage, Medicaid, Medicare, TRICARE, (Health insurance program provided to retirees, active duty members, retirees, reserve & activated guard members, and families) and specific other coverage.

- **Patient's Bill of Rights:** The bill assists all American citizens with pre-existing conditions to acquire and maintain their health care coverage. The bill also protects citizens' choice of doctor, finishes lifetime limits received by consumers, and encompasses other provisions.

- **Review of Insurance Rates:** Notably, this is part of several reforms seeking to enhance insurers' responsibility and consumer limpidity. The rate review intends to help the insurers keep their costs down and to hold the insurance companies accountable. It helps protect the insurers from unreasonable rate increases by requiring insurance companies to publicly explain any 10% or more increase in the insurance rates before raising their premium.

- **Student Health Plan:** These are health insurance coverage offered by universities and colleges to students when family coverage is unavailable. A fully insured student health plan is one that the university or college purchases from an insurance company. Some of these plans are comprehensive, while others offer limited coverage. Unlike other health insurance options, the student health plan allows for the grouping of the premium costs with other related higher education expenses such as board, room, and tuition.

ACA brought intense changes for small employers, as well as the market where they buy packages. Nevertheless, the effect of ACA provision is the ability to enhance coverage choices and reduce administrative costs for small employers, diminished by the convenience of non-compliant plans, not to mention other beneficial provisions. Studying the small-group market trends by reviewing premium and enrollment data, as well as federal and state policy choices, remains imperative. Therefore, the focus in this market review is on six states in the United States to include Minnesota, Arkansas, New Mexico, Montana, Vermont, and Pennsylvania.

Small Group Market Trends

The ACA insulates the health insurance market from price hikes. ACA made the health insurance market robust. Nonetheless, the significant evolution it is undergoing remains evident. Notably, small-groups refer to organizations with less than 50 employees. Stakeholders in different studies in the listed states offered insight into trends in the small-group market, which may characterize the nationwide market.

Premium trends and offer rates. The small-group market experienced low and moderate rate augmentations between 2016 and 2017. Minnesota, Arkansas, Montana, and Vermont reported some decline in the number of small employers who offered group health plans. The number was less than anticipated.

Shift to and from the individual market. Most small businesses, especially those with less than 10 employees, abandoned their group policies and shifted their workers to the individual market in 2014. Nevertheless, many of the employers shifted to the small-group market because premiums are on the rise again and provider networks are narrowing. Hence, the individual market's less than generous coverage causes a shift and doubt over the prospect of ACA.

Stretched coverage decisions for small businesses. ACA introduces an environment with expanded coverage options for the small business proprietor, especially those whose employees are young and healthy. As such, most small employers have been in provisional *grandmother* plans ACA non-compliant in states that continue to permit them. Nonetheless, enrollment is on the decline for those groups whose health is in decline change to ACA-submissive market. Steadily, enrollment declined or disappeared entirely in *grandfathered* plans.

Level-funded yields sold to healthier groups. The insurers changed the marketing of level-funded products that mix self-funding, administrative services, and a stop-loss plan. The products target small businesses with relatively young and healthy employees. The products are cheaper for these groups than ACA-compliant policies. As these plans gain power, they will divide the market between low- and high-risk groups.

Supplementary purchasing provisions for small groups. There are emergent groups purchasing arrangements aimed to appeal to small employers with healthy workers. These include self-funded group captives and MEWAs.

Health compensation arrangement (HRAs). Representatives of small businesses, as well as brokers, reported that HRAs are a potentially attractive coverage option for most small business proprietors. They will help workers buy individual health insurance but are yet to acquire much of a foothold in the marketplace.

Discussion

For some small businesses, those with more than 50 employees, ACA enhanced premiums rates. However, some with young and healthy workers encountered premium hikes. Brokers and insurers quickly responded to these employer groups. Moreover, government policies allowed a wider variety of coverage options than ACA originally envisioned.

- New options for coverage can increase affordability for employers with healthy employees. Nonetheless, they are likely to pose a risk to the small-group market as a whole. Upon the division of the markets between healthy and less-healthy groups, there will be a rise in premiums for the latter group; thus, the number of insurers willing to offer them coverage will reduce.

- Many new products aimed at catering for the young and healthy necessitate small employers' entry into complex monetary arrangements, which can expose them to new financial and legal risks.

- State and federal legislators have the aptitude to monitor data on evolving coverage choices, as well as their effect on premium trends. They can respond with policies supportive of all small business purchasers.

National Trends on Offers and Enrollment Rates

Countrywide, the share of small businesses that provided health insurance between 2011 and 2015, reduced from approximately 36% of the total U.S. small businesses to below 30%. Within the same time frame, the enrollment rates, the percentage of small business workers using their employers' insurance offer, decreased by a more modest 2.7%.

Premiums: National Trends

According to the Agency for Healthcare Research and Quality (AHRQ, 2017), premiums for personal or family insurance coverage by small employers increased slowly since the passage of ACA. Compared to year 2010, before the introduction of ACA. The rise in average premium was approximately 3.1% per annum between 2011 and 2015. By contrast, the premium rose at a higher rate between 2005 and 2010. Specifically, the premiums went up by approximately 4.4% for single coverage and 5.6% for family coverage. Furthermore, the small group market's rate of increase tracked the enhancement in health expenditures countrywide, with the large-group marketplace and Medicare included.

ACA and the Small-group Market: Key Reforms

Insurance reforms in ACA included a major focus on a dysfunctional individual market. As a result, policymakers sought to address some of the inadequacies of the small group market. These included the lack of insurance sets, as well as high and frequently volatile premiums for numerous small businesses because of year-to-year inconsistency in an employer group's position.

Insurance Reforms

Many states formerly set consumer protection principles for premiums and profits in the small-group market. However, ACA introduced a set of all-inclusive standards at the federal level applicable to small-groups and individual markets. The reforms included:

- New rating guidelines that prohibited insurers from using health status to set premium rates while setting the limit on the quantity charged based on employees' age.

- The lowest set of essential profits based on what a typical employer-based plan offers, as well as a prerequisite to cover preventive service without sharing cost for enrollees.

- A ban on limits on exclusion from plan profits based on pre-existing situations.

- An annual cap on the number of employees required to pay for the out-of-pocket costs, counting deductibles, coinsurance, and co-payments.

Notably, the law exempts employers with 50 or fewer employees from fines and penalties for failure to offer affordable and enough coverage to workers. However, ACA requires employers with more than 50 employees to provide minimum level coverage or pay penalties.

SHOP Marketplaces, Health Reimbursement Arrangements, and Small Tax Credit

ACA led to the creation of new and state-based marketplaces called Small Business Health Options Programs (SHOPs). The purpose of the SHOP was to respond to apprehensions among small employers on the limited obtainability of insurance options, as well as the inability to deliver the employees' choice of health plans. Therefore, ACA developed the small business premium tax credit with middle-income employees enrolled through the program. Notably, the tax credits are only obtainable for 3 years. Despite the considerable participation of insurers in the SHOP run by states, created in the District of Colombia and 18 states, SHOP has considerably lagged expectations. In 2016, the Obama administrative established a rule to rescind an earlier prerequisite that major insurers take part in federally managed SHOPs. Resultantly, most of the insurers declined in participation between 2017 and 2018.

CHAPTER 9

The Relationship Between ACA and Small Businesses

The proposal by the U.S. Congress to repeal and replace ACA prompted Americans to ask questions with regard to whether its good intent makes the ACT useful in the healthcare and business professions to improve the lives of Americans. ACA influences both large and small corporations in their occupational levels. Most business owners either have an incorrect comprehension of the sole purpose of the provision or prefer the traditional method of healthcare coverage. Either way, the Act is both supported and opposed by different members of the U.S. Congress and changes are underway. While the provision affects both the small for-profit and not-for-profit organization in a similar fashion, some Americans believe that they should be treated differently.

The focus remains on the method of calculating the working hours of the full-time equivalent (FTE) employees as provided by ACA's mandate. As such, the Small Business Health Options Program (SHOP) applies to corporations with less than 25 FTE employees. The option allows small companies providing health plans to offer one choice to their workers. The SHOP has arguably expediently aided small business in providing health and dental insurance to their workers. According to a survey of 700 proprietors and potential buyers done by BizBuy Sell 2017, 420 respondents wanted President Donald Trump to address the issue rapidly. The purpose of the article is to deliver an extensive explanation of the impacts of the PPACA on small business and healthcare.

ACA PROGRAMS AND PLANS: IMPACTS ON SMALL BUSINESSES

The Small Business Health Options Program (SHOP)

Small businesses take part in ACA through the Small Business Health Options Program (SHOP), which intends to deliver health and dental coverage to workers in small organizations. Since January 1, 2018, small employers enrolled through private insurance entities as well. Also, some continue to make use of SHOP-registered brokers or agents. In short, the SHOP plans are the only prerequisite methods for a small business health care tax credit to reduce premium cost. However, small employers suffer at the hands of other health care law requirements. For instance, ACA requires that small employers report or rather provide certain information to their employees regarding the marketplace. Notably, small employers should do so whether they offer health insurance.

The Affordable Care Act positively impacts small corporations with less than 50 FTE workers because they pay only 50% tax credit on their employees' insurance premium cost. Further, these businesses can procure health insurance for their workforces through the SHOP. The intention of the program was to be a separate health care exchange for minor corporations to facilitate the ability to offer employees diverse choices when picking a plan. Nevertheless, the establishment of The ACA postponed the program until 2015. The postponement means that small companies providing health plans can only provide one option to their workers. Those who initially supported the Act were upset after this decree. According to an advocacy group known as the *Small Business Majority*, the delay was an enormous misfortune for small companies. Thus, health insurance remains a significant concern for small firms based on affordability and availability.

SHOP helped small business provide health and dental

insurance to their workers amenably and expediently. As mentioned, the requirement for a company to purchase the insurance is to have 1-50 employees. An eligible company does not have to wait for the Open Enrollment Period. As such, the employers can begin offering SHOP coverage to their employers at any time of the year. However, SHOP is for firms that have at least one full-time equivalent (FTE) worker excluding the owners, family members, or partners. SHOP provides choice and agility whereby the proprietor can convey one plan to their employees or allow them to choose from many. Similarly, the program provides either health coverage or dental coverage or both. Employers choose the amount to pay for the worker's premium and whether to provide insurance to their dependents. Employees are free to choose how long new workers must wait before registering. Notably, the SHOP program is a major boost to small businesses because of increases to employee participation.

Summary of Benefits and Coverage (SBC) Disclosure Rules

Since its formation in 2013, the Affordable Care Act has been at the center of examination and has had abundant impacts on Small Businesses. ACA requires employers who provide health insurance to their employees should provide the health insurance to all eligible employees within 90 days after starting their employment. Employers provide their workers with a regular summary of benefit and coverage (SBC) form which explains the health plan coverage and its costs. The SBC helps workers comprehend their insurance options. Employers who fail to do so are likely to be fined on non-compliance grounds.

Employees will not contribute more than $2,650 to their annual Flexible Spending Accounts (FSAs) in the tax year 2018. Notably, the limit does not encompass employer contributions to the employee's FSAs. In 2017, the U.S. Treasury Department and the IRS gave notice altering the enduring *use-or-lose* rule for FSAs. FSAs are benefit plans that business proprietors can sponsor to enable their workers' reimbursement on a tax-favored basis for medical bills that employers do not cover in their major medical plan. In the United States, approximately 14 million families take part in health FSAs. The employers offer plans together with other benefits. However, employees normally fund them through contributions by means of voluntary salary reductions. The FSA's exclude contributions in the employee's revenue.

The ACA's Impacts on For-Profit and Not-for-Profit Organizations

While deliberating the issue indicates the commercial effects, the discrepancy between the effect of ACA on both for-profit and not-for-profit firms is vital. In other words, the Act altered the way employers offered motivation to their employees. For instance, small for-profit organizations embarked on a decision to reduce working hours while others changed the incentives offered.

After the enactment of the regulation, many people did not expect that the act to cause an upsurge in the cost of business. For example, there has been an increase in the healthcare bonuses and associated fees such as the Patient-Centered Outcome Research Trust Fund fees, as well as reinsurance fee. ACA associated regulatory burdens affect the cost of employer-sponsored health care plans. The costs have implications for employees and employers. However, no clear indication exists whether there were any jobs lost. Similarly, it is unclear whether the law caused any delays in small organizations expanding their employee count. A clear argument exists that some of the small for-profit agencies had to reduce the benefits that they offer to employees because of cost. Employees working less than 30 hours in a week no longer receive benefits.

Therefore, Obamacare seems to lower the cost of healthcare to businesses. However, it is still having not achieved the intended objective. The objective of candidate Barrack Obama's campaign promises of lowering health insurance premiums and overall health care costs, which is the intended objective envisaged during its enactment. Thus, it became clearer ACA impacts the value of business negatively.

During the institution of ACA, most non-profit organizations hoped that they would be safe regardless of their size. However, non-profit organizations noted that ACA requires large organizations, including the nonprofit companies, to provide their employees with minimum and affordable coverage; citing penalties for failure to doing so. It is worth noting that ACA does not contain any exceptions for the nonprofit organizations regardless of their financial status. Nevertheless, most of these organizations take advantage because the law excludes small agencies. By excluding a small company, the rule applies to all employers with at least 50 full-time employees. The rule impacts nonprofit organizations that exceed the threshold of 50 full-time employees. Increased expenditures hinder the accomplishments of the small nonprofit organization.

Impacts on Business and Health Financial Management

Importantly, ACA has had a massive effect on the hospital financial management. For example, meeting the expanding consumer needs necessitates an increase in the amount of health insurance premiums. Therefore, financial management staff played a vital role in ensuring the profitability of the Act, as well as making possible both the patient and healthcare givers benefit. In other words, financial management staff promoted changes related to expenditure, reimbursement, and cost of care. Compensation is one of the essential aspects of the healthcare financial management.

Avery, Finegold, and Whitman (2016) emphatically hinted that Obamacare Act decrees that all citizens are beneficiaries of healthcare coverage and there is a general notion that ACA should decrease the costs.

Business owners ought to propose provisions that call for an increase in quality of care and increase revenue while reducing cost. The owners are responsible to call for the rise in the minimum number of workers to meet the requirement of the Act. Agreeably, ACA significantly changed the reimbursement in the healthcare sector. However, the quality of care provides reimbursement of equal or better value than a specific set of the fee; it is possible to have increased the cost of care as time moves forward.

The Act decreed that large organizations are the ones affected and penalized if they do not do as required by law. However, small businesses remain concerned that irrespective of their size, they ought to use audits as a preliminary strategy. In the past, there were challenges in medical billing because of the inaccuracy of entered billing codes. ACA should have rules and regulations that increase the importance of medical billing codes. For instance, the finance management staffs in small businesses, especially in health care, are supposed to complete a Medicare Risk Adjustment (MRA) audit to provide compliance with all medical coding. The staff is required to audit each member in the company. Notably, the audit information is crucial; without it, financial staff cannot plan budgets founded on contemporary and historical data. The issue to address is the lack of highly specialized software to complete the task professionally.

Individual Mandate and Non-compliance Penalties

The U.S. Supreme Court sustained the constitutionality of ACA's individual mandate approving the fine imposed by ACA to businesses that fail to procure health insurance. The U.S. Supreme

Court held that it is a legal exercise of the U.S. Congress' authority to tax. ACA required American citizens to obtain by Jan. 1, 2014 either a private health plan or health cover via a state exchange in case they were not then relieved or covered by their firms. The obligation does not apply to Americans aged 65 and above because they are under the Medicare program. The consequences directed by the IRS, are pro-rated depending on the number of months within the year that healthcare does not cover a certain individual. However, there are no fines if a person is uninsured for less than 3 months. Starting 2015, insurance corporations started sending their plan applicants and the IRS a form confirming that they had complied with the ACA provision on employee insurance coverage. ACA required taxpayers to attach the IRS form to the tax forms.

For the 2014 tax year, the penalty for the entire year was $95 per adult and $47.50 per child, up to a family maximum of $290. Notably, the penalty is equal to 1% of the family's income. In 2015, the quantities augmented to $327 for every adult, $162.50 for every child, and a family all-out of $980, which is 2% of the family's revenue. For 2016 and successive years, the full penalties estimate at $695 for every adult, $347.50 for every child, and a family all-out of $2,085, which is approximately 2.5% of the family's earnings. The CBO's approximations were that 4 million individuals will select to reimburse the fines instead of buying coverage. In 2018, the CBO's approximation seems accurate at the time of this writing as most younger Americans with no children and in good health did not opt for coverage.

Particular individuals are exempted from the coverage prerequuisite. These comprise undocumented refugees, incarcerated individuals, Indian tribes' members, and people surviving between jobs and have no insurance for more than 3 months. As such, people with certain religious objections, as well as those who calculate that their premiums will be greater than 8% of their family income. Particular credits, which would be expanded from the lowest-quality campaigns in their state's fitness give-and-take, will be exempted from the coverage obligation and the consequences. Last, persons and families with income below $9,500 per year will be exempted from the penalty for not purchasing the health insurance. ACA provides that Americans whose income ranges between $9,500 and $37,000 per year will be subject to a penalty of $695 per person.

By contrast, experts use a different formula to calculate the penalty for Americans who earn more than $37,000 per year and do not hold the health insurance coverage. Based on the formula, the penalty for Americans with the income of $50,000, $75,000, $100,000, $125,000, $150,000, $175,000, $200,000 and over $200,000 and do not demonstrate that they hold the health insurance coverage incur the following fines: $1,000, $1,600, $2,250, $2,900, $3,500, $4,100, $4,700, and the cost of a *bronze* health-insurance plan respectively.

Taxation statements include a question regarding whether an individual has medical health insurance in effect throughout the year. Most of the times, employers, insurance firms, and the exchanges send data directly to the IRS, but each tax filer needs to answer the question every year. The particular question appears on 2017 tax returns, just as indicated in years 2014 through 2016; there is no difference under Trump management. Enforcement is stricter for 2017 taxation statements than it has already been in previous years. Regarding the 1st time, IRS suggests that filer may be at liberty to leave the question about medical health insurance empty. In prior years, one could bypass the insurance question entirely. Avoidance is no longer an option. In addition, intentionally falsely reporting to the IRS is against the law, so more filers face accountability dilemmas proving whether they obtained coverage in 2017. Regarding most unpaid fees, there are a number of methods through which the IRS can recover their money. The text of ACA is very clear that taxpayers who fail to pay their ACA fine are certainly are subject to prices, liens, or legal prosecution.

In January 2017, the IRS conveyed that 6.5 million taxpayers reported a total of $3 billion U.S. dollars in ACA fine payments for 2015. However, more than 12.7 million people were uninsured and certified for an exclusion from the penalty. The average charges amount was approximately $470, with an average penalty of around $330. Therefore, the average penalties are much lower than the average refunds that taxpayers expect, such that it is easy for the IRS to simply subtract the charges from the refund. The IRS observed that for 2015 revenues, 77% of the filers with outstanding penalties still received refunds after the penalty deduction. The average penalty was somewhat higher in 2015 than in 2014 (it was $210 on average for that year). The penalty augmented again in 2016, on the levy returns submitted in 2017. Yet for 2017 and 2018, the charges remained unrevised from 2016.

ACA demanded adjustment for inflation of the flat-rate fine every year after 2016, but the IRS confirmed no regulations for 2017 or 2018. The penalty continues to be 2.5% of the salary or $695 per uninsured individual and $347.50 for every uninsured kid up to $2,085 for every family. As such, the penalty does not increase and 2018 is the final year the fine applies. For most of the individuals, the penalties remain lower than the average refundable amount. The IRS can acquire the fines by simply concealing the penalty from the filers' reimbursement checks. For filers not owed a reimbursement in a particular year, the fine can be taken from a future year's recompense instead. Notably, if one structures their taxes such that they always owe money and never get a repayment, the IRS includes payments to filers' oldest arrears first. Consequently, in an upcoming year, filer's tax payment apply to a previous year's penalty, instead of the income tax they owe for the year.

In December 2017, the tax modification bill, known as the Tax Cuts and Jobs Act, passed the U.S. Senate, as well as the House of Representatives. President Donald Trump ordered the tax cut into law later in 2018. Notably, the tax reform bill makes substantial changes to the national tax code. The bill does not influence the mainstream of ACA tax provisions. Nevertheless, it reduces ACA's distinct shared responsibility, also called individual mandate, fine to zero, effective at the start of 2019. Resultantly, starting in 2019, individuals will not be penalized any longer for failure to obtain suitable health insurance coverage. While the tax reform bill eradicates the individual mandate of ACA's fine, the repeal does not gain effect until 2019. People must obey the mandate or pay a fine for 2017 and 2018. Failure to acquire suitable health insurance coverage for these years might lead to a fine. Once becoming a law, the tax reform bill will reduce the ACA's individual obligation fine to zero, effective in 2019 tax year. ACA efficiently abolishes the individual requirement fine for the 2019 tax year going forward. Therefore, starting with the 2019 tax year, people will not be penalized any longer regarding the lack of suitable health insurance coverage for them and members of their family.

CHAPTER 10

Opposition and Support
for ACA

Regardless of these positive changes brought about by ACA, the larger majority of U.S. citizens still oppose. Americans oppose the directive that everyone must have to purchase health insurance and they are at odds with the government role in medical care. Yet the U.S. community overwhelmingly accepted Medicare, which is an obligatory insurance for aging people that the national government controls since 1965. The disagreement with some government obligations in medical care finds a foundation the common people do not trust the U.S. government.

The devastatingly negative TV advertisements contrary to ACA by the Republican candidates in the 2012 and 2014 elections had a key influence on Americans' opinions regarding ACA. Approximately 60% of Americans indicated much of information they have on ACA was from watching TV. Disagreement with the U.S. government's role in healthcare, as well as about compulsory health insurance that makes it improbable that the United States will be capable of ensuring all its people have continuing access to healthcare in the near future.

A small minority of the U.S. voters, approximately 17%, support the Republican program to repeal and substitute key parts of Obamacare, while 56% of them criticize the bill, which is likely to end up in a do-or-die vote, according to a new poll in 2017*. Additionally, the Quinnipiac University poll revealed that 46% of voters stated they will be less likely to vote in their U.S. senator or congressman election if they go for the replacement of the GOP plan. Around 19% claimed they would vote for their representatives under similar circumstances. Also, 29% of voters said their congressperson's vote would not matter. The poll further decreed that 1 out of every 7 Americans considers the possible loss of their health coverage if the bill passed.

Elements of ACA that the Public Support

The features of ACA that were well-thought-out to be auspicious in a Kaiser poll in December 2011 and an NYT-CBS poll (KFF, 2011; The New York Times, 2012). The only element disapproved in ACA was the directive that all citizens ought to have health insurance or face penalties. Delegated health insurance is not a new thing in the United States; Medicare is one of the mandated health insurances in the U.S. adults managed by the national government since 1965.

The Partisan Divide

Democrat and Republican approaches towards ACA in a 2014 poll depicts that ACA remains a highly partisan issue. As revealed in the 2014 poll, 83% of Republicans disagreed with ACA, while 56% preferred abolishment. Contrastingly, only 19% of Democrats opposed it, and only 4% desired its abolition. The discussion surrounding the expansion of Medicare coverage, as well as Medicaid for the last 40 years, remains highly political. A Democratic House and a Democratic Senate passed the Medicare bill which a Democratic President signed into law. The approval of Medicare expansion likely has an impact on the outcome of the poll.

In another 2014 poll, 41% of American citizens asserted that it is the federal government's responsibility to provide all Americans access medical care insurance coverage. In short, 12% of the Republicans agreed, compared to 70% of the Democrats.

Therefore, one reason why so many Americans criticize ACA is their mistrust towards the government and its role in healthcare. Moreover, the percentage of citizens who have faith in the federal government dwindled from 78% to 24% between 1964 and 2014. Several polls demonstrated that Republicans are far less trusting of the government compared to Democrats. Results of these polls suggests that criticism of ACA by Americans may largely along party lines. The argument is in line with the results of the 2014 CNN / ORC poll (Cable News Network [CNN], 2014). In this poll, 7% of Republicans asserted that they trust the government to perform duties most or every time, while only 23% of the Democrats made the same assertion. Worth emphasizing that CNN conducted the poll at a time when President Obama was in office which suggests skewed views towards party lines.

Why Republicans Hate Obamacare

Some Republicans referred to ACA as "the most dangerous piece of legislation ever passed." Other people claim that it is vicious to personal and individual freedoms or call it the "Fugitive Slave Law." Republican lawmakers, who are the sources of these quotes, affirm that ACA is an appalling law. Since the Democratic U.S. Congress passed ACA, it has been the Republicans' bête noire. The party has been pushing more than 60 ineffective Congressional votes to reverse; therefore, forcing the Supreme Court to debate it on four occasions in the Act's short history. Additionally, ACA was also at the core of the 2013 two-week government shutdown. Therefore, it begs the question, why ACA attracts such excoriation from the right.

Republican aversion emanates from economic, ideological, and historical reasons. Ideologically, the central mechanism behind ACA is that Americans who manage to pay for coverage straight from a supplier are charged higher premiums so as to aid payment for the grants delivered to those who purchase their insurance from government-run markets. As such, it is the kind of redistributive economics that is an abhorrence to small government. Many purists, for instance Tom Price, the Health Secretary in Donald Trump's administration, see the drive for collective coverage as an indication of the U.S. government interfering with the private doctor-patient rapport.

Subsequently, purists claim that ACA's economics fail to stack up. While it seems contentious, the number of Americans deprived of health insurance reduced from around 16% to 11% from 2010 to 2016, according to Gallup's (year) research. Statistics advocated that the uninsured populace among low-income White people who have no college degree dropped from 25% to 15% in 2013 to 2015. A large number of people who voted for President Trump are among the main recipients of Obamacare. Also, premiums rose in 2017, by a mean of 22%. Many brokers lost cash on the exchanges as clients were older and sicker than they expected. Insurers, in turn, passed on the cost to better-off Americans. The Republicans' argument has been that ACA represents the commencements of market catastrophe: higher prices will daunt healthy and young American citizens from signing up; such insurers will make additional losses. As such, prices might rise again until the system breaks down.

Last, many citizens view ACA as the state-of-the-art round in a multi-generational battle against healthcare proffered by the state. In his early days as president, in 1945, Harry Truman proposed an enlargement of the current obligatory social coverage system to encompass health care for all American citizens. The AMA was entirely against, and its PR firm created the perfect expression to sink it: *socialized medicine.* In 1946, when the Republicans gained control of the U.S. Congress, the policy dropped. The government used disruptions of tax to stimulate firms to deliver private indemnification plans. Workers acquired them and health-care provision became entangled with employment. Subsequent presidents from the Democratic Party including Johnson, Clinton, and Obama pushed the U.S. government further in the direction of universal healthcare delivery. The tag of socialized medicine spread as fast to ACA as it did to Truman's strategy and may well resurrect again in 2019.

CHAPTER 11

The Relationship Between Business and Healthcare Insurance Law

In 2015, Oregon health brokers lost red ink as the unrelenting struggle in the industry and in relation to ACA continued. The combined losses of the state's seven main insurers almost multiplied to $164 million, whereby distressed Moda Health Plans alone lost close to $50 million in a high-profile financial disintegration. Meanwhile, the state's hospitals solely enjoy ACA revenue and big profits. The hospitals' assistance care plunged since the Act passed into law, which also led to the augmentation of their 2015 turnover precincts compared to 2013. The hospitals' achieved a bonanza at the taxpayers' expense, not to mention the insurance firms, as well as clients who, in some ways, face double-digit coverage premium rate increments.

Many people, for instance, Jack Friedman, former Providence Health Plan's chief executive (CEO), asserted that it is the providers who benefit from ACA. After 18 months since the breakthrough Affordable Care Act began, the legislation prospered in its prime goal: offering 16.4 million, previously uninsured American citizens, insurance coverage. In Oregon, over half a million individuals acquired coverage via Medicaid or marketable insurance by the use of the newly created exchange. Nonetheless, that attainment has been challenging, discernable by technological glitches, partisan resentment, and financial problems. Numbers released in 2015 by the state of Oregon's Consumer and Business Affairs Department indicated that Oregon insurers paid a price as they struggled to adjust to the vicissitudes.

Unexpectedly, Providence Health Plan, rather than Moda, dispatched the biggest losses of the year compared to the other big seven players. In 2015, the Providence Health Plan lost $63 million, which was a drastic decline from the $22.3 million profit posted in 2014. Gary Walker, PHP's spokesman, accredited the big loss to an incursion of expensive new consumers and a misguided 14% cut it applied in 2015. The firm reported a vast capital reserve, approximately 1,000% over state requirements. In 2013, Moda lost approximately $49.5 million. The exertions of the second-largest carrier in the state was known in the country. The carrier's push into the discrete market created by ACA attested a financial tragedy, which worsened when the U.S. federal government failed to deliver promised financial aid.

Questions about Moda's endurance eddied around the corporation for months until regulators of insurance Oregon took started supervising the company supervision. The state affirmed that it would start the procedure of helping Moda clients move to diverse, stronger indemnification companies. Thirteen days afterward, the Moda narrative took another bizarre twist when the state abruptly withdrew its order of regulation. Oregon agreed to allow Moda to recommence business as usual and continue with its strategy to stock up its capital reserves with $170 million in new funds. Seemingly, Moda already initiated $43 million of the new money. In the financial statement delivered by Moda in 2015, the firm unveiled that in December, it borrowed an extra $43 million from allied companies. The amount was an addition of $50 million the firm borrowed from its parent company in November, as well as another $50 million borrowed from OHSU in 2014.

Moda officials declined to comment on the story, same as Laura Cali, Oregon Insurance Commissioner. Blue Cross was the only firm among the big seven health carriers in Oregon to post a turnover in 2015. The Portland-based company netted $25.8 million in that year, notwithstanding what the firm's President Angela

Dowling referred to as "perplexing financial and regulatory alterations in our industry." By contrast, Pacific Source lost $10 million, Health Net Plan lost $25.5 million, LifeWise lost $35 million, and Kaiser lost $13 million. A wave of amalgamation currently ongoing in the health coverage business and most anticipate it to gather steam in the face of comparable pecuniary struggles across the business. Health Net already merged with Centene Corp., based in St. Louis.

The Upsetting Economics of ACA

Looking back, prior to passing ACA, healthcare yielded high rates. Citizens who were poor could not sustain consistent coverage, but small business did not have challenges managing premium payments for their employees. Maybe the world's most byzantine prearrangement of doctors, clinics, hospitals, pharmaceutical companies, contractors, private and public insurers, pharmaceutical companies, medical schools, nursing homes, and numerous other stakeholders typically works well, and America's doctors precisely work round the clock and are, therefore, highly regarded in the healthcare setting. Nonetheless, fusing these incongruent components to make an intelligible health economy often looks similar to alchemy than science. ACA is arguably the most contemporary effort at transfiguring the portions of healthcare into a well-operating entity. However, it is evident that Aetna's unexpected exit from health-insurance exchanges of the state and predictions in coverage premiums resulted in a serious reservation on the probabilities of that responsibility succeeding. Doubts emerge questioning whether the exit is a result of turbulent implementation of ACA or just an indication of an incomplete implementation of ACA because of the pressure of impossibility.

Provision of care in the American healthcare system is costly, but it does not adhere to typical supply and demand curves for some reason. For instance, health indemnification shields most patients from direct charges because the government plays a role in controlling the health insurance market. However, insurance is a chief supplier to the irreconcilability of accessibility and affordability. In many insurance markets, the motivation is for insurers to recompense for as minimal things as probable in exchange for even, definite premiums. For instance, life insurance's is possibly the ideal indemnity market. Nevertheless, the fact that everybody will die is inevitable. Yet, death is a highly probable event for older individuals, as well as those with certain disorders and behaviors, such as smoking. Therefore, a life insurer would never take on an enrollee who is obviously about to die. As such, insurers deprive clients of their dividends or insurance entirely based on their risk factors.

American health plans drive the health-insurance marketplace further from denying susceptible patients' insurance. Healthcare coverage itself never arose in a perfect market, because soon after its commencement, it developed into a recruiting tool for proprietors. The wide anticipation of health indemnification in the working class, not to mention an emergent health-care scheme engrossed on offering pre-emptive and primary care services, destined that indemnity had to cover routine services afar the calamitous events with which the definitive insurance model is well-matched. Tax inducements in the 1940s and 1950s made employer-sponsored indemnity, in which firms and employees often divided risk costs, fundamentally the pillar of American healthcare and delivered inexpensive services for many of the middle-class people.

That expansion permitted insurers to tap into immense, stable populaces of healthy adults supported by the steadiness of their employers' assistance, and the subsequent windfalls aided in the creation of the modern American system. The expansion premised on a group of doctors and infirmary that depend on workers and pensioners' rich reimbursements to counterbalance losses from poorer, sicker, and uninsured patients. Since the 1950s, the majority of the money-makers in indemnification risk pools have been arranged. Every healthcare reform stage in the United States has ever since involved a momentous investment of public tax money to bring accessibility and affordability closer and closer to fruition, while maintaining the rudimentary premium-based model in its rightful place.

In 1965, the establishment of Medicare and Medicaid delivered government-sponsored medical protection nets to three of the most vulnerable groups: people with disabilities, elderly people, and poor families that have children. After that, the 1986 Emergency Medical Treatment and Labor Act prolonged the Medicare authority by demanding that any healthcare facility that accepted its patients and their payments to offer appropriate medical screening examination and treatment to any patient with a medical emergency, notwithstanding of their aptitude to pay. The Children's Health Insurance Program, also referred to as CHIP, ominously extended Medicaid's pool to low-income people with children in 1997.

The main issue with that tactic is continually questioned. Evidently, it is costly for the government, because of taking on the outlays of jeopardies and arguably bloated health-care expenditures. The financial argument for widespread coverage is that indemnifying everybody will cause a healthy amalgam of sick and healthy people to stabilize risk. Moreover, indemnification will endorse the use of inexpensive preventative care that lessens the need for costly treatments in future. Yet, those are downstream objectives with substantial price tags. Obamacare premises on that fiscal argument, initially in search of universal indemnification by strengthening private coverage via exchanges and employers run by the state. Moreover, the objective is to extend Medicaid suitability to healthy adults with low-income and without children, not to mention provide supports to anyone left out. Last, ACA necessitates and compels people to buy insurance and business owners to provide the health insurance coverage. Each of those stages required complex tax-code amendments and frequently shifted the expenses of risk to the central government, which projected to amount to more than $130 billion to secure those alterations.

So far, the state coverage exchanges are the parts of ACA that have been the toughest to implement. People without cheap employer coverage or public coverage have the aptitude to shop for tiered, often-subsidized covers and ACA provides that people should do so by the individual mandate. The unending issues with both demonstrate just how problematic reform can be. The formation of a strong self-purchase indemnification market was vital to providing coverage to these people. Nonetheless, states and the federal government in turns made errors with the exchanges. Several states basically declined to cooperate, compelling the federal administration to cover the expense and create the time to generate exchanges that could accommodate local populations. Other states, for instance, Oregon, struggled too much that federal commissioners had to step in nevertheless. The national rollout of the HealthCare.gov sign-up portal was a total disaster, and sign-ups unrelentingly lagged for years. At that point, Aetna withdrew from the insurance exchanges.

The states' health protection exchanges are a somewhat small piece of the coverage pie—only around 12.7 million individuals acquired exchange plans by the time the latest open enrollment period ended. Employer insurance dwarfed the exchanges by comparison. But the individuals targeted by these marketplaces are the most inscrutable and hard for insurers to cover. Often, they earn too much to be eligible for Medicaid, although they are underemployed or under the middle-class. In layman language, they are habitually a mix of *young invincible* commonly fit and do not see a high essence for coverage. They include an older, sicker workforces who are either unwaged or work in smaller companies for part-time jobs and need insurance but cannot afford it and are ineligible for Medicare. To incentivize the group to register, ACA depends on a carrot and a stick analogy. As the carrot, ACA offers robust subsidizations based on the exchange's plan charges and income for individuals above Medicaid aptness who earn less than four times the poverty line. Moreover, the punishment if you do not register is a tax directive to purchase coverage.

Up to this point, the carrot is much more effective compared to the stick, and that is not a promising thing for the markets. Notably, the sickest older qualified people largely signed up for profoundly subsidized health coverage, while the fit younger people have been unwilling until lately. New rules barring insurers from denying coverage or adjusting premiums based on rudiments of risk have destined that they either garner losses, increase premiums, or do both in the event that their patients become sicker than anticipated. These two options (i.e., garnering losses and increasing premiums) seem to be taking place in tandem, and the exchange benchmark plans' premiums will augment by approximately 10% on average by 2019 as a result. The augmentation will not be a huge problem for many people in the marketplace, as over 80% of all enrollees do not essentially see the true expenses of coverage. Notably, federal tax acclaims applied to premiums, expense-sharing of copays, deductibles, and coinsurance between the federal government and patients resulted in the failure to see coverage expenses. Nonetheless, it is a U.S. federal government and insurers' problem.

In a bid to control premiums and prevent death spiral while aggregating costs and patient risk both ceaselessly intensify each other, ACA offers additional coverage, risk alteration, and *risk corridors* to recompense insurers who cover sicker recipients and experience higher expenses than expected. Essentially, the programs spread the whole individual market's gains, as well as those of insurers that covered lower-risk patients, to lessen the losses of the ones with sicker enrollees or higher costs than estimated.

The programs ought to have performed as substitutes, momentarily inspiring individual-exchange insurers to use their fair share of sicker recipients. While these unethical practices direct billions to insurers that have withstood losses in the market, risk passages and reinsurance go away, and risk hallways have been far behind on outlays that insurers started a class-action litigation in February 2017 to seek recompense.

It is not surprising, then, that Aetna lost more than $430 million since entering into the exchanges. In a similar way, Aetna made a resolution to vacate all but a minority of exchange marketplaces. Aetna cited matters with the risk pool. The risk pool matters involved the sicker patients entering compared to healthy patients. While that foundation was undoubtedly doubtful given the publication of documents signifying Aetna exit from the markets in reprisal after the Department of Justice blocked a merger with Humana, the move had an indisputable financial rationality behind it, particularly for an insurer the size of Aetna. As such, it begs the question on the need to partake in an expensive individual market when the profitable employer plans, privately-controlled Medicaid plans, and Medicare advantage are up for grabs.

Although Aetna's move climaxes major subjects in the exchanges, the move undoubtedly is not a calamity for Obamacare. Recipient in the federal insurance market, articulated confidence in the marketplaces after the move and in a blog post distinguished that the exchange risk pools are in additionally acquiring healthier, lower-cost clients in the long run. Government supports help steady the market. Adversative selection is unlikely to cause the dreaded death spiral of ever-augmenting charges and ever-sickening patient cores. Because indispensable covered reimbursements are homogeneous under ACA, plans can compete by reducing the costs and aggregating the efficiency of the services they offer. Early returns from lucrative insurers show that the strategy is working.

Despite the exchanges having underwent losses of close to

$3 billion in 2014 and were on the correct path for bigger losses through 2015, a McKinsey report demonstrated that carriers receiving an affirmative margin in 2014 seem to share some common factors, plus narrowed systems and managed plan design. Kaiser HMO plans seemed to be key recipients of that market penchant, and several Blue Cross plans abandoned some fewer limiting choices for managed attention. In the wake of Aetna's withdrawal, Blue Cross plans essentially articulated confidence in their aptitude to manage care, as well as expand into new circumstances. Given time, there is an indication that exchange marketplaces will self-correct and several models that positively draw in stable risk pools and lessen adverse selection. However, that self-correction would inexorably end in high-profile broker withdrawals like Aetna's, which was essentially part of the plan.

Health-care reformers cannot afford to wait for that self-correction because plan exits like Aetna's put people at the mercy of an inherently volatile environment and run the risk of violating Obama's central pitch about keeping plans. They run the risk of making Obamacare easy political fodder for Republican campaigners. Pinal County, Arizona, remain without any exchange insurers after Aetna's withdrawal next year, and roughly a quarter of all counties in the country are already left with only one option. While most people will not feel the effects of plan exits until next year and do not shoulder the burden of premium increases, premiums have gone up for many families and any dysfunctions in the controversial reforms are easy political targets. Counihan signaled that exchanges will aggressively recruit insurers for 2017 to ameliorate the attrition. He suggested that the administration will fine-tune its risk-adjustment strategy to better deal with high-risk patients and will open doors for states like Alaska to address specific market needs with program waivers.

Those are fairly minor tweaks though, and even several champions of the 2010 law continue to push for major changes to health law. The public option seems to have received most traction after Aetna's exit, and it still polls favorably among most Americans, despite exclusion from the original health-reform debate early on. Private insurers, states, nonprofit organizations, or a mixture of each across the United States possess the ability to administer the public option. Tax dollars backstopped the public option and would guarantee the existence of at least one market-proof option in every county and state, all the while siphoning off some of the riskiest components of the exchange pools. Proponents cited the size and bargaining power of the federal government, as well as the resulting efficiency and market competition when making the case for the public option. It is still unclear if that theorized bargaining power and efficiency would be able to fix the risky problem in the exchange markets, however.

One possible fix to those risk pools could be simply restoring the original form and function of ACA. Expanded Medicaid intends to use federal and state funds to cover all people under the federal poverty line. However, the Supreme Court decision in NFIB v. Sebelius gave states an opt-out for Expanded Medicaid. Nineteen states chose not to expand Medicaid, and in those nineteen states, the floor for exchange subsidies reduced to the poverty line, which ACA does not force people to purchase health insurance. The reduction places approximately two million people, who would be eligible for Medicaid, into exchange markets. The lower-income participants are likely to be sicker than participants in the intended risk pools.

Of the 18 states that had the worst exchange performance among insurers in the McKinsey (year) report, 12 did not expand Medicaid to all low-income adults and three expanded the program after the exchanges went live. One of the remaining three was Oregon, where the $200 million debacles of the health-insurance-exchange implementation may have had long-term effects on sign-ups of healthy people. A choice by states to expand Medicaid as intended, perhaps in combination with a plan such as Hillary Clinton's *Medicare for More* plan, which would extend Medicare buy-in options for people over 55, could help balance risk in the exchange markets and put the sickest patients into government-managed health care.

Preventive Health Care Services Under ACA

Whereas the main goal of ACA is to increase access to the old health care system through the development of inexpensive health insurance opportunities, there are precise provisions that develop access to both primary and secondary deterrence services including vaccinations and consistent disease screening. Many health plans require preventive services to members devoid of copayment or coinsurance expense even irrespective of unmet yearly deductible so long as the services are provided within the network of the plan. Preventive health services encompassed on the surefire list include cancer screenings, for instance, colonoscopies and mammograms, cholesterol and blood pressure screenings, not to mention adults and youth immunization (e.g., flu, mumps, and measles,). Numerous behavioral health involvements are cost-free, including alcohol abuse screening and counseling, screening for depression, and tobacco cessation therapy and interventions. ACA entails free delivery of Food and Drug Administration-ratified contraceptive approaches. Nonetheless, the access is intricate for employers with a spiritual opposition to contraception.

Impact of ACA on Healthcare Workforce

The Affordable Care Act has a large effect on healthcare employment, a development feared to extend into the future. Increasing pressure on demand for doctors, nurses, healthcare practitioners and other healthcare workers has been realized because the growth of freshly insured patients. Situations surrounding the creation of the present transformational setting in the healthcare industry have magnified the workforce effect of ACA. ACA came at a period when the middle U.S. citizen was growing older, a trend happening currently and will carry on for decades. As healthcare consumption grows with age, the getting old populace will require healthcare specialists to attend to them. Additionally, the healthcare professionals that attend them are growing older, resulting in retirements in the face of increasing demand for clinicians. Inclusively, the refining economy escalates demand for healthcare provisions as citizens are financially stable and can afford deductibles and co-pays because of the healthcare benefits. Therefore, the demand for healthcare services overawed the supply of specialists owing to a combination of the above-mentioned forces. Since the enactment of ACA, meeting the demand has been a major problem.

Implications of New Care Settings on the Workforce

The workforce demand and supply imbalance is affected by ACA implementation. The following are the main ways:

✓ ACA further added about 20 million new patients to the spools of the insured population since the full enactment of the Act in 2014. The increase in the number of healthcare clients adversely resulted in an increasing demand for healthcare services as the new consumers started using their insurance. According to AMN Healthcare, an increased demand for nurses, therapists, technologists, technicians, and other healthcare specialists began to thwart in mid-2014. The demand health professionals gradually resulted in an increasing gap between doctor demand and supply. The breach between healthcare job hires and job overtures have advanced since 2014.

✓ ACA incentivizes populace healthcare and cost suppression

alongside the progressively competitive healthcare industry. The uplifting of the existing profiles and creation of new roles due to the market and regulatory changes have changed the workforce. For instance, home health requires skilled therapists and nurses owing to its fast growth as an industry. Additionally, a new team of experts, normally registered nurses with professional training, executed integrated care. In addition, owing to the competitive and regulatory developments in the revolution of health information technology, there has been an alarming requirement for health information managers, medical programmers, and other technologists.

✓ The rise in the patient care call is a long-term phenomenon, which can be attributed to ACA. Therefore, the attribute has led to the uplift in the demand for workers as the health insurers refer to the clienteles as protected lives. The increasing demand for the healthcare experts will be broad-minded and cumulative, as the already insured will be forever covered for the rest of their lives according to the laws of the land. Apparently, as the new insurance members grow older, they will require specialized healthcare with time. ACA can be blamed for the increased ultimatum for healthcare professionals that are being experienced by the healthcare system.

✓ In association with the current competitive structure, adverse demand to rapidly fill the leadership positions, whether everlasting or temporary hires, is critical. Concurrently, new leadership positions such as chief experience officer, chief clinical transformation officer, and chief populace health officer among others were established. There is an alarming escalating demand for leaders in the healthcare sector, similar to other professional roles. For instance, its broadly notable that a leadership vacancy is very unfavorable to quality, tactical planning and attractiveness at a health enterprise in the healthcare industry.

It is projected that the forces influencing present healthcare workforce demand and supply discrepancy will continue for proceeding years. Even if these changes in healthcare are linked to ACA, many other aspects have amplified them. Most notably, nothing can be reversed to reverse the problems being experienced because of the intensifying petition for healthcare experts who range from the nurses to hospital chief executive officers. ACA effects on healthcare have raised several questions, which include; With regard to increased demand for care, how many suppliers will be desirable, in what topographical dissemination, that is, countryside, peripheral or urban and in what title roles? In addition, what are the personal delivery replicas that will deliver excellent, competent, effective, and cheap care, at the same time, meeting the wishes of patients within inhabitants across a well-defined geography, both regularly and in tragedies? The present labor force is faced with numerous problems. However, ACA introduced opportunities for the extended roles, new-fangled directions, and teaching needs to complement prolonged scopes of carrying outs and to establish complete accessibility of care across suppliers in a calamity.

Fresh care provision models exist to provide the mounting number of protected individuals looking for care in the new archetype of value-based refund. A consideration is the common communal paramedics who answer 911 calls and deliver immediate care on-site. Then, they refer the patients to alternate care locations except for the Emergency Department(ED). Also, there are intensivists, who are new providers, who are medical doctors that exercise outside the hospitals with the aim of enhancing care after hospital discharge in a bid to minimize readmissions. Minute clinics, exigent care centers managed by insurers, independent EDs not affiliated to hospitals and many others are examples of delocalized care sets designed to provide care to individuals at their locations. Telemedicine is also in use, with the characterization of the capability of remote consultation and patient care provision, in calamities and consistently.

Assessment of the Current and Future Health Care Workers

The United States has about 15 million health care benefactors, which represents about 15% U.S. jobs, according to Ani Turner. Approximately 30% are based in hospitals, nursing, and residential care account for greater than 20%, while around 45% work in different ambulatory sets. Approximately 30% of that labor force exclude the health care providers. The healthcare provider workforce is experiencing a serious deficit of health experts and may continue to the next decade. ACA breaches the assurances of access and eminence of care for all Americans by intensifying the deficiency and growing the problem and pressure on the system. ACA's efforts to solve the deficiency provide no proof and narrow in range, and the substantial financial outlay will not produce an outcome for years owing to the preparation pipeline. With ACA's approximated 190 million hours of book-keeping annually enacted on the health care sector and businesses, with a combination of deficiencies of personnel, patients will face restricted access to medics, increasing wait periods, reduced time with attendees, and reduced satisfaction. The healthcare workers will experience increased strain and unsteadiness, and a main restructure of the labor force is desirable to spread care to the millions of Americans.

The future healthcare workforce faces a critical system overload. Bottled up demand from the Americans waiting for medical cards and fascinated by the assurance of *free* or endowed care is projected. Undoubtedly, physicians, nurses, and other health specialists want to assist patients in need, but the absolute logistics of extended care provision, the existing and rising scarcity of workers, and insufficient resources will definitely challenge the good objectives of the legislators who came up with the state health law. Actually, the *transformative* changes pushed by the law's supporters will probably obscure and undesirably shake health care providers and their capacity to deliver care. These alterations will intensify regulatory problems, increase already weighty loads, cause a reduction in payments, enforce new fines, and neglect personal likings and standards. The increased strain will further weaken the healthcare sector. A combination of these factors will impend access and superiority of care countrywide, thus breaching the President's guarantees and the aforementioned intentions of the Americans in the U.S. Congress involved in the implementation of the national health law.

On taking a deep analysis of the population demographics, the present U.S populace is greater than 315 million and it is projected to continue increasing. Estimation is made that by 2030, 72 million Americans will be above 65 years, which accounts for a 50% change in age demographics since 2000. The change could be attributed to the people who were born during the last period of the World War II. Because of the advancements in medical technology and highly improved care administration, Americans are having a longer lifespan than ever before. Senior citizens represent 12% of the population, which will make up 21% by the year 2050. The increasing inhabitants will lead to a rise in chronic diseases and further stress on the healthcare workers.

The scenario seems to make a bad situation worse. Currently, there exists a distribution imbalance. In many parts of the country, health professionals tend to be largely concentrated in urban areas. In pursuit of the Congressional enactment of Health Professions Educational Assistance Act, to add the number of the healthcare workforce in the countryside and underserved areas, the government recognized Health Professional Shortage Areas (HPSAs) in 1976. However, the result remains unachieved because the access to care is still imbalanced between rural and urban areas all over the United States. There is a need for approximately 8000 primary care doctors in countryside areas and deficiencies of therapists and dentists according to the U.S. Department of Health and Human Services (HHS). Great inequality can be noted, taking into account that a quarter of America's residents live in rural and suburban areas, yet only 18% percent of nurse practitioners and 10% percent of doctor's work in those areas. Rural inhabitants are poorer and have high chances of participating in federal government aid, creating the potential for extraordinary demand due to the enlargement of Medicaid in 26 states. Geographical constraints affect the well-being of rural Americans via prolonged wait periods, long-distance travel because of difficulties in accessing care and inadequate resources.

ACA then initiated favorable terms and conditions in a bid to solve the misdistribution problem. ACA increased financial support for the Public Health Service, funded workforce planning, restructured loan payment and forgiveness, and increased Medicare-funded Graduate Medical Education (GME) and introduced sponsorships and scholarships. The purpose was to reduce the rural shortages, but only minimal success seems to have been achieved through them. The worry is the inadequacy will lead to heightened ill health and mortality among the rural inhabitants. The solution to the problem will include an instant change in educational admission practices, payment restructurings in the private and public areas, employment of laborers with rural familiarities and an improved regulatory environment for medical exercise with an inclusion of a tort reform. As can be seen, ACA came with health reforms which seemed favorable and appealing to the eye, but which impacted negatively on the citizens located in the countryside and suburban areas.

Another labor force problem is the unbalanced ratio of prime care physicians to professionals. In the healthiest states, research shows that the idyllic ratio of primary care physicians to professionals is

50% to 40%. Presently, a big gap exists, with a third of the doctors practicing in primary care. Inferior quality of care and increased medical costs is a characteristic of nations with higher ratios of professionals to primary care doctors. TACA puts emphasis on free preventive care and the idea of the Patient-Centred Medical Home (PCMH) prototype. Nevertheless, these models still need sufficient primary care providers to provide services. Clearly, the issue presents difficulties considering the present and anticipated personnel inadequacy. To satisfy the needs of the newly protected populace under ACA, there is a need for a minimum of 8000 supplementary primary care doctors. There are predictable deficiencies of between 20,400 to 45,000 primary care doctors in the next years despite the use of physician assistants and nurse practitioners.

There is a need for upper intensity of care. The higher the patient acuity, which is an extent of the intensity of care needed to take care of a patient, the more attention a patient needs. In relation to workflow, the implication is that the number of health specialists required to care for a patient is dependent on the nature or magnitude of the patient's medical illness. As projected, the number of patients ailing from chronic maladies will increase tremendously as Americans age. Consequently, America will definitely require extra working hours to provide quality care. Moreover, the chronic illnesses are not only affecting the elderly but the young Americans. Research depicts that by 2025; there will be a rise in demand on the healthcare sector as almost half of America's inhabitants will be suffering from a terminal disease.

Further, the imminent retirements tend to complicate ACA's goal achievement because of the elderly population and aging workforce. A third of the estimated 985,375 physicians and 2.8 million registered nurses presently working, will retire in the coming decade. Predictions in the workforce show that there will be a perilous scarcity ranging between 91,500 to 130,000 doctors. The requirement for a supplementary 300,000 to 1.2 million nurses by 2020. The practitioners stayed in the workforce for monetary reasons because of the economic decline of recent years, but the increased pressure of the ACA will probably encourage their evacuation. A 2018 labor force survey conducted by the Association of American Medical Colleges (AAMC) indicated that physicians who are over 50 years of age are devoted and meticulous compared to the younger ones who are less meticulous, disillusioned, and less devoted. The younger doctors show diverse arrogances toward their professional duties and responsibilities. According to the survey by the AAMC, 2017 (Markit, 2017). According to the data in the AAMC survey, physician productivity will decrease with an increase in retirements.

Variability in the scope of practice cannot be left behind. In 2010, the Institute of Medicine (IOM) put out a report recommending that all nurses practice to their full capacity depending on their teaching and education. Advanced Practice Registered Nurses (APRNs) are well-versed professionals who provide services in several specialties. Currently, the laws on the scope of practice vary greatly between countries. Some allow complete practice by APRNs without supervision by physicians; others recommend minimal practice by only allowing APRNs to work in close supervision by a physician while some limit practice with the requirement of oversight, observation, and partnership with a physician. Conversely, the insufficiency in the workforce will force nations to amend their scope of practice laws.

The educational pipeline merits consideration, as presently, medical education institutes lack the ability of graduating the number of employees required to assure broad access to health care. Despite the current increase in enrolment, the supply will be outdone by the demand by 2025. Qualified candidates cannot access admission to professional schools since the educational pipeline is backlogged. Factors that contribute to the refusal of qualified candidates in the professional schools include budgetary restraints, inadequate clinical sites and a limited number of trainers. Medicare-funded GME slots are scarce to finish the training course despite the increasing enrolment by medical schools. The American Association of Medical Colleges is in support of legislation to upturn Medicare-sponsored slots. The absence of residency apertures precludes graduates from practicing medicine despite the ability of medical schools to graduate more candidates.

Stress Aggravated on Healthcare Workforce by ACA

The quality of patient care cannot improve without better working conditions in which the strong and growing medical staff can work. Many health practitioners prefer other careers and opportunities because of the impact of ACA on their performance. ACA intensified stress on the different workers, systems, and administrations by overburdening them with the complex requirement to implement the colossal law. ACA requires them to oblige to the legal obligations while meeting professional prerequisites for excellent performance in administering patient care. ACA, therefore, exaggerates these health problems rather than solving them. Ever than before the heavier workloads experienced by medical workers has made it difficult to maintain enough ratios, which can warrant quality care without any difficulties. Negative outcomes accrued to the hefty workloads and workforce pressure include upsurge of medical blunders from exhaustion and even undesired outcomes that may include the death of the patients. If a substantial investment of human capital is not accomplished to meet the escalated number of patients, ACA will put pressure on the already over-pressured medical professionals.

Since 2015, surveys show frustration and exhaustion by those working in health care. The frustration can be caused by the surge of work –interrelated pressure which affects the workers' emotional and mental well-being. Data showed that 60% of the physicians would not commend medicine as a profession and that a third of them would not take medicine if given an option to do it again. Doctor wellness was associated with the capacity to provide high-quality care to patients. Americans may face additional labor losses since the increase in physician discontentment may lead the doctors to leave the profession. There is evidence as a recent survey indicated that 49% of physicians intended to leave the medicine field soonest possible or lessen the period they work in the field. The practitioner's tiredness from work overload and emotional strain has led to their discontentment thereby threatening restructuring exertions and patients' care access. For the nurses, workstation pressure leads to tiredness and depression which results in absenteeism thus increasing the work load on other nurses. The nursing teams work in short-staffed and overloaded units which leads to emotional distress causing high turnover.

The medical practitioners lack the right of conscience. These practitioners fear about their previous ability to execute their rights of integrity under ACA, as they are keen on the virtuous and moral issues that emerge occasionally in the healthcare field. For the time being, the administration deliberately ignored right of conscience by commanding funding of contraception, sterilization, and abortion-inducing drugs. Even though the moral concerns are wider, the supporters focus on the reproductive and the unborn baby rights. Additionally, ACA regulation presents a barricade to Medicaid doctor-patient relationship via the Independent Payment Advisory Board outlining what treatments should be financed hence determining the permissible treatments. The side-lining of practitioners brought about by ACA regulation overlooks safety and oversteps on the moral and acceptable obligations defined by the medical professions. Without well-defined legal protections, health care personnel might be forced to decide between dropping their occupations and holding on their individual ethical and moral beliefs.

Solutions to the Problems Faced by the Workforce

The threefold aim of improved quality and satisfaction, subsidized costs, and improved health can only be assured with an effective workforce big enough to accommodate the requirements of an aging and developing population. Lasting resolutions to the prevailing problems will require invention in medical training and edification, improvement of care delivery and execution of policies to maintain the prevailing healthcare personnel. Education improvement will be help to the workforce and the conditions of learning should be the obligation of the occupations. To make medical practice appealing, legislators should address some tenacious problems such as restriction of misdemeanor burden and other constrictions generated by the debt burden after the graduation of personnel from the medical schools. Medical and professional colleges ought to embrace admittances measures that charm students from rural regions and the course should address the complications of practice in a suburban setting. Medical professionals should also include interprofessional learning to enhance output and efficacy, support harmonization of care, and have training drills in teamwork. The unbalanced ratio of medical workforce and misdistribution should be addressed to improve worker output and realize high competence through premeditated planning.

Another resolution will be to endorse efficient care delivery and improve the working environment. Because human capital is the pillar of the medical care industry, enrolment and retaining of the adequate labor force are of importance. To enhance workflow and healthcare coordination, professionals ought to collaborate and endorse teamwork. The labor force insufficiency obliges healthcare leaders to innovate new methods to use the inadequate employees proficiently to meet the heightened demands. Retaining ability will involve widespread human resource organization and incentivizing over workforce safeguards, remunerations, education and career improvement, and revenue sharing. Quick solutions to avoid overburdening and tactics for stress control will lessen tiredness and exorbitant replacements and guarantee satisfactory supply. To warrant a vigorous workforce, workers need to be secure emotionally, bodily and psychosomatically. Last, the practitioners should have the right of conscience and should not be enforced to choose between executing their ethical integrity and following possibly corrupt orders of their seniors.

The Predicted Future of Medical Sector in the Balance

The success of excellent medical care under ACA is in doubt. The employee's inadequacy, which can be traced to the practices that preceded ACA, seems not any better by the new health law. If the shortage is carried on, it will become a hindrance to the victory of ACA and will destroy the quality of health care of Americans. In a snapshot, the United States needs more nurses, physicians, and other medical practitioners. Under the ACA, the government has discussed further detailing its role in medical care financing, but instant and direct funding affect the provision of healthcare and accessibility to care in general. The effect does not depict the quality of care. One must consider the characterization by meager care quality, restricted or no access to care, and increased wait times. Sensible reforms in medical care laws should be made without affecting the care of the majority. The core problem should be carefully examined and dealt with amicably. Conclusively, ACA's unplanned implications can no longer be overlooked, as Americans should have the right to freedom in medical care. For the realization of better and the planned intentions of ACA, the U.S. Congress must revisit this law and make the appropriate amendments.

New initiatives: The Prevention and Public Health Fund and the National Prevention Strategy

ACA unambiguously established two initiatives to endorse public health and prevention through the Prevention and Public Health Fund (PPHF), as well as the National Prevention Strategy (NPS). PPHF is a source of funding started to provide extended and unrelenting federal stashes in research; reconnaissance and tracking; and communal health organization, workforce, and teaching. Devoted funding aids in ensuring that public health, as well as healthcare systems, are not in competition with other departments in the government for limited resources. Additionally, the PPHF underwrites to several programs, encompassing the National Prevention Strategy, and grants that are based locally, for instance, the Community Transformation Grant, as well as the National Public Health Improvement Initiative.

The NPS targeted at the Surgeon General together with other stakeholders, such as the heads of seventeen federal agencies and also the public. The overarching objective was to increase the number of citizen with good health at every life stage. The NPS recognizes four strategic guidelines and seven tactical primacies in order to enhance the health of every American citizen. There are several recommended programs, policies, and systematic methodologies for each strategic course and priority.

The main strategic direction example is empowered people whose emphases is on evolving and executing ways of supporting people in energetically handling their own health. The approach takes into consideration many of the obstacles to the creation of knowledgeable health decisions, such as excessively multifaceted health information and a shortage of communal health-supportive funds. To check on these apprehensions, the central government remains dedicated to backing up future exploration on health literateness and stronger communication with the community based on the Plain Writing Act. Empowered People recommended that suppliers find new means of sharing serious health info with patients and confirm their understanding level. In addition, community partners support adults' health education and help generate healthy surroundings for the ease of performing activities.

Efforts to attain the objectives defined in the NPS are primarily ongoing, together with America's Great Outdoors Initiative, which a community-based method of seeking long-term conservation resolutions. Also, the NPS objectives are in line with those of the Neighborhood Revitalization Initiative, which is an inter-federal organization initiative for helping regions in anguish transform into neighborhoods of opportunity.

The Prevention and Public Health Fund has, therefore, delivered possessions to two distinguished initiatives: the National Public Health Improvement Initiative (NPHII) and Community Transformation Grants (CTGs). CTGs, presented through the Centers for Disease Control (CDC), offers communities the assets to grow and devise creativities to thwart chronic disease and to aid in the distribution of best practices. For instance, Maryland grantees use CTG funds to combat tobacco use, develop tobacco-free societies, and lessen passive smoke exposure. The NPHII started with the objective of improving delivery of care and augmenting system capacity. The initiative aids health departments all over the country in enhancing performance and safeguarding a new national endorsement. In 2013, for instance, NPHII delivered fund amounting to $32.4 million to 73 state, local, tribal, and territorial health divisions.

Other ACA Strategies for Improving Public Health

Various prospects of ACA advance public health. As such, the Internal Revenue Service (IRS) necessitates the performance of a community health needs assessment (CHNA) by non-profit hospitals after three years and delivery of annual reports on the degree to which they are handling identified requirements. While local community health departments have undertaken CHNAs for many years, ACA prerequisites generate an opportunity for hospitals, as well as health departments, to team up on the valuation and enhancement of public health.

ACA correspondingly necessitates the enactment of a National Quality Strategy. Significantly, the strategy has three goals: affordable care; improved health care, and *Healthy People, Healthy Communities*, which concentrates on refining the U.S. population health by backing up verified interventions to sort social, behavioral, and environmental elements of health. Also, the National Quality Strategy launches six priorities to endorse quality healthcare, such that two of the six priorities have distinct implications for enhancing public health. First, the National Quality Strategy promotes the most operational prevention and treatment procedures for the principal causes of death. Second, it works with communities to endorse the universal use of superlative practices that enable healthy living.

CHAPTER 12

The Evolving Federal-State Partnership

The Affordable Care Act remains contingent on states as the primary units delivering oversight and implementation of the new principles for health insurance trades, benefit design, and premium rates. The law shaped new prospects of state DOIs, along with the chance to apply for national grants and sustain their extended role. Even with the grants, applying and imposing the voluminous new insurance standards introduced by ACA is tranquil for state DOIs. For instance, federal procedures necessitating insurers to offer policies to children under the age of nineteen, irrespective of a health condition, made many insurers to proclaim they would not sell "child only" policies any longer in 2010. Notably, the policies meant that families would buy an indemnity policy at any cost for their kids. While that ensued, the District of Columbia (DC) and 22 states replied with new regulations or guidance to insurance brokers to certify that child only insurance would still be accessible to families that required the insurance policy. The actions proved that, in most cases, states had suppleness to react to market variability and engross with insurers, as well as other impacted stakeholders in ways that the national government cannot.

ACA forced several new states' demands, extending their ability and expertise in better ways. For instance, conventions instigating the ACA's Essential Health Benefit (EHB) standard requested states to entitle a statewide benchmark strategy used as an insurers' reference point of reference when trade small-group and individual market plans.

ACA requested DOIs to enlarge the range of their plan and rate review. For instance, preceding ACA, many DOIs evaluated network sufficiency for only HMOs, and then habitually only when the insurer firstly sought an HMO authorization. Only several states did annual appraisals of the supplier networks for all the plans accessible in the market. Nevertheless, ACA projected that the state marketplaces or exchanges would yearly review and confirm that plans partaking on the ACA's markets meet system suitability standards. Similarly, the ACA firstly established a nationwide exclusion on prejudiced benefit enterprise. The enterprise means that insurers couldn't set benefits or cost-sharing any longer, especially in ways that discriminate against enrollees on the basis of disability, age, gender or life expectancy. Although state DOIs traditionally studied health plan agreements to ascertain that they cover state required reimbursements, evaluating the whole benefits package for probably biased design is, for many DOIs, an entirely new activity.

President Trump's government indicated that they will use a hands-off tactic to insurance company lapse than taken by the Obama administration. An Executive Order in January 2017 directed Health and Human Service (HHS) department, as well as other federal agencies to deliver increased suppleness to the states to produce a "more liberal and open healthcare market" and also use all "power and option" [to "defer, waive, and grant exemptions from, or delay the enactment of"] ACA provisions that might execute a fiscal or supervisory burden on insurers, individuals or states. Since Executive Order publication, HHS officials have, for example:

- **Relaxed registration and benefit design necessities on insurance companies.** New federal guidelines confirmed in April 2017 made it easier for insurers to reject covering people who cannot document aptness for distinct enrollment chances or those who previously failed to pay premiums. The rule offers insurers better suppleness to enforce deductibles or other charge sharing than permissible under the Obama's government.

- **Delegated oversight responsibility to the states.** During the Obama administration, HHS executives appraised plan networks for those states that submitted to the central government for the process of the health insurance market. New HHS dogma stated that as long as a state possesses the *authority and ways* to conduct health plan networks evaluations, the federal government is bound to accept its documentation that they are satisfactory.

- **Shortened timeframes for a government review of health plan premium rates and forms.** HHS deferred previously recognized time limit for insurers to submit their market plans for assessment and accreditation, leaving less time for national and state officials to conduct full reviews.

- **Extended the life of non-ACA compliant health plans.** Rules in the Obama administration permitted people and small employers to refurbish plans that did not meet ACA necessities through 2017. HHS dispensed a delay of the strategy through 2018.

- **Solicited public input on ways to reduce health plan regulatory burdens.** Through an official *Request for Information*, HHS implored propositions for organizational paths to increase consumers' health plan adoptions, decrease the insurance cost, and confirm the customary monitoring authority of the states. In light of these and other actions by federal officials, states must regulate how the alterations impact their errands to protect clients and certify the conservation of stable, operation of local coverage markets.

The federal managerial discretion scope may be extensive and can range from real-world rulemaking that is likely to unwind strategic morals or protections in the Obama era to decide to selectively avoid enforcing particular necessities on insurance providers or recipients. Below is a discussion on the five areas whereby the Trump administration wants to change ACA policy, their impending effects, and the power and implements, both regulatory and statutory, that are obtainable to states to react to the changes. The strategy is not a conversation of possible national legislative accomplishment to alter the statute, nor is it a comprehensive review of the entire probable areas in which the Trump administration could administratively change health insurance ideals or the procedure of coverage markets. The narrow set of cases below exemplifies the extent, as well as the limits, of state power to accomplish their coverage markets and protect clients.

Health Profits: New Suppleness for Insurers

Before the establishment of ACA, health coverage plans traded on the individual market frequently omitted handling of critical services. For instance, 1 of 5 adults in an individual plan required medicament drug coverage. States authorized to a certain level some coverage for particular services, but these values differed broadly, leaving most clients deprived of access to inclusive benefits packages. Within the individual market, 19 states only required coverage of mental health care, and twelve states only required maternity care coverage. In states that endorsed the consumer safeguards as well, individuals frequently had high cost-sharing, lifetime and yearly subsidy limits that constrained access to lifesaving care and precautionary services. ACA's EHB necessities wish to provide health insurance is inclusive and increase the access to health care.

ACA introduced a list of 10 EHB groupings that all non-grandfathered plans sold in the individual and also small-group markets ought to cover, ranging from laboratory amenities to childbearing and neonatal care. The law additionally guides HHS to describe the EHB as equal to the scope of reimbursements provided under a characteristic employer plan. While ACA offers a clear track on the EHB classifications that insurers have to cover, it gives the HHS Secretary the authority to regulate the particular details of remunerations included in every category. The Obama administration introduced flexibility into states to describe the EHB by selecting from ten prevailing plans to regulate a benefit benchmark. Other health plans derive from the benefit benchmark. Although states may enforce coverage requirements that surpass the EHB, they must cover the price of supplementary benefit mandates.

Redefining Essential Health Benefits

Only the U.S. Congress can eradicate either of the 10 subsidies categories necessitated by ACA; yet, the law guides the HHS Secretary to occasionally *update* the EHB. Also, HHS officers reinforced reduction of the scope of aids insurers have to cover, and offering insurers with better litheness to design plan remunerations. HHS, Under Secretary Price, surmounted back EHB oversight, complying with the state determinations to assess prescription drug formularies, as well as cost sharing for bigoted benefit design.

Current guidelines necessitate insurers to deliver remunerations that are *considerably equal* to an EHB-benchmark plan of a state. The government reserves the right to modernize the basics in the requirements and could try to decrease the generality of essential benefits in every category. The Obama administration used executive power to increase benefits further than the base benchmark plan in each state. For instance, in 2013, when instigating the EHB benchmark tactic, they discovered that facilitative amenities do not reflect benchmark plans.

The administration provided states with the preliminary chance to control encompassing that category; if states didn't express the scope of insurance, insurers remained accountable for deciding the services that their plans ought to cover to obey the facilitative service requirements. Additionally, the Obama administration used rulemaking to enhance substance to the category of prescription drugs benefit category. Federal procedures oblige insurers to first establish at least one drug in every U.S. Pharmacopeia (USP) category (i.e., at least one type of insulin and one non-steroidal and anti-inflammatory drug). Second, the insurers include the obligation to create a review team to safeguard that the list of covered medications is recurrently rationalized. Third, they ought to provide for an exemptions procedure in case an enrollee requires access to uninsured drug. The current administration has comparable suppleness to regulate how the definitions of the EHB

Issues for Consumers and State Options

In the event that HHS modifies the EHB necessities, for instance by providing insurers better tractability to assure lesser treatments or services in the ten coverage groupings, insurers may use that tractability to design yields that discount coverage of particular health services, meritoriously discouraging enrollment among clients who need the services. While diluting coverage for such services as hospitalization or prescription drugs may lower expenses for some people, clients who still want comprehensive services coverage in that given EHB category face fewer opportunities and increased prices.

States implemented for protecting customers and safeguarding comprehensive coverage via state-level implementation and directive of the insurance market. While anticipating likely federal deregulation, states might codify the existing EHB requirements into their individual insurance codes. In their 2017 statutory sessions, Hawaii passed, while Rhode Island and Nevada established bills, for purposes of codifying the 10 categories EHB. Also, in

2017, New York Governor, Andrew Cuomo, directed his Financial Services Department to issue protocols *protecting* the EHB categories.

Several states started the process of codifying the 10 EHB benefit categories while implementing the ACA. By contrast, states such as California and Washington set the 10 categories to form law and indulged insurers to provide guidelines corresponding to a benchmark plan in a state. Notably, the aids in ensuring unremitting coverage of an all-inclusive kind of services in each category if the management withdraws the necessity that insurance providers adhere to existing EHB definitions. Even without the need to codify the EHB or a standard plan, most state DOIs have current authority to fill federal requirement gaps and make sure that benefit designs ascertain the enrollees' health care needs. For instance, if the management withdraws rules used in the Obama era, necessitating insurers' coverage of at least one prescription drug in every USP category, states may step in to warrant formularies cover an adequate amount of drugs in numerous categories and classes.

Relaxing Federal Oversight: Giving Back Plan Management to the States

The law provides that the health insurance markets of ACA's should engross in five key utilities: determine aptness for national financial aid, enroll buyers into qualified health plans (QHPs), conduct plan supervision, provide consumer aid, and do financial management. The ACA drafters intended that most states would create their own market and conduct the above-mentioned functions. Nevertheless, by the time marketplaces launched in 2014, 17 states only took on full accountability for operating their marketplace and executing all the mentioned functions. Moreover, 33 chose to use a federally facilitated marketplace (FFM). However, 17 FFM states have begun *plan management*, which embraces the

QHPs certification, reviewing and assembling rate and benefit info, handling contracts with QHPs, checking current compliance matters, recertifying and decertifying QHPs, not to mention handling open and special matriculation periods. Although state DOIs can give recommendations for QHPs certification or recertification, under the law, the marketplace is the one obliged to make the final resolution of a QHP's appropriateness to participate. Hence, in the FFMs case, HHS is the *decider*.

In the process of running the FFM, Obama's government administration fortified states to do plan management tasks; where that happened, HHS largely deferred to the judgment of states about QHPs. Conversely, federal administrators took their eventual accountability seriously for QHP accreditation and requested insurers to succumb data on rate and plan to HHS, which conducted its individual plan analysis. For instance, in the wake of buyer and provider fears regarding excessively narrow supplier networks among QHPs, Obama's HHS started requiring from insurers submission of lists of suppliers partaking in their QHPs and conducting its assessments.

A New Approach to Management of Marketplace Plan

Going forward, president Trump's administration will no longer conduct network competence appraisals in states with the means and ability to do them. More broadly, HHS has indicated that they will streamline further the QHP accreditation procedure by further deferring to states' assessments of plans and proportions in assistance to the states. Explicitly, HHS has avowed it will no longer:

- Consider whether QHP insurers are accredited and in perfect standing in their individual states;

- Conduct QHPs network sufficiency reviews in a state with the *authority and means* to do that;

- Evaluate QHP's service areas (within states that perform plan management); and

- Evaluate the formularies or benefit designs of QHP's prescription drug to determine whether they discriminate according to individuals' health requirements and other factors (in the states that perform plan management).

For the above-mentioned activities, HHS will consent states' endorsements. Nevertheless, in states that do not carry out QHP plan administration, HHS will carry on with its own evaluations of plan service extents, benefit designs, and formularies.

Issues for Consumers and State Options

Probable federal lawmaking and managerial actions impend the future feasibility of ACA's markets. Consumers registered in marketplace plans are to continue depending on government oversight to make sure they obtain the full array of safeguards assured by federal and state law. For instance, many insurers will probably to continue pushing the envelope in the direction of narrower provider networks so as to provide economical premiums. Although many buyers revealed readiness to trade broad choice of suppliers for a subordinate price, exceedingly narrow networks might interrupt their capability to access care promptly.

As such, new rules prevailing in marketplace registration and an insight that the ACA's individual mandate won't be compulsory may give some insurers augmented inducements to use services, benefit designs, and drug formulary to deter registration among high-risk populaces. Notably, these incentives demand to monitor oversight to certify that all insurers in the markets are playing similar rules and that individuals with preexistent conditions can acquire insurance that meets their requirements.

Recommendations

Increasing Affordability

Affordability in healthcare increasing through ACA by reducing out-of-pocket limits and cost-sharing and improving minimum employer coverage requirements. The U.S. Congress ought to consider modifying ACA to increase eligibility for cost-sharing decrease payments and cut out-of-pocket restrictions for moderate-income people or families. The U.S. Congress or the Trump administration should also consider improving least indispensable coverage and least value requirements to make sure workers acquire at least a minimum degree of safety from worker's coverage. Consequently, these improvements may increase the insurance affordability for millions of American citizens. Increasing the use of health savings accounts among moderate-income Americans is imperative in augmenting affordability. The U.S. Congress ought to align the requirements of ACA, as well as the health savings account initiative and ponder over offering supports for health savings accounts among moderate-income American individuals and their families. As such, the strategy could reduce healthcare expenses for innumerable moderate-income Americans.

Through allowing the use of health reimbursement accounts to procure health insurance, the U.S. Congress ought to amend the IRS Code to permit small employers to make use of health reimbursement accounts. Moreover, the small businesses should do so with suitable protections, to aid the workers in purchasing health coverage. Incorporation of value-based coverage design to sustain indemnification for high-value services is an imperative strategy for enhancing affordability. The ACA necessitates insurance providers to repay clinical precautionary services minus patient cost-sharing if the services earn an *A* or *B* assessment by the U.S. Preventive Services Task Force. Similarly, expert bodies could demand coverage of high-value secondary deterrence and disease control services from the public and private insurers without copayments and deductibles.

It is crucial to enhance state directive of network and formulary sufficiency. States ought to adopt a regulation or modify existing ones to ascertain that insurer systems and formularies are suitable and evenhanded. Moreover, control over networks is a genuine tactic to governing health care charges and safeguarding provider quality. Nonetheless, networks ought to be delimited to certify the plan enrollee has access to required care and are not distinguished because of their medical situations. Lastly, improvement of protection from balance billing is of the essence in the bid to increase affordability. States should espouse statute to defend network plan enrollees of balance billing as they access to care in predicaments or via network providers. Importantly, the move is obligatory in ensuring that enrollees of a network plan avoid assessment of huge medical bills when they fail to pursue care out of network.

Improving the Consumer Marketplace Experience

The active guidance to clients during the selection of coverage is vital. The marketplaces ought to provide superior tools, and individual assistance, to customers to select plans. The strategy may help make sure that clients willingly enroll in the plans that are suited to their requirements and possessions. Improvement of the network and formulary limpidity is crucial; the markets and state officials ought to demand better network and formulary transparency from insurance providers and set up tools to aid customer better comprehend the networks and formularies accessible to them. Hence, the strategy might aid in ensuring admittance to suitable care and continuity of care for clients.

Standardize Insurance Products

Marketplaces need to homogenize products offered by their insurers. As such, the homogenization would enable and advance both the consumer choice as well as insurer competition.

Allow the Use of Health Reimbursement Accounts to Buy Health Insurance

The thing to consider when allowing small business owners to finance health refund accounts (HRAs) drawn by employees is small businesses obtaining medical insurance in the personal market. Notably, the allowance is presently illegitimate under ACA's government interpretations, as well as preexisting tax regulation. Employees may require legal protection to make sure that employers deal with all workers the same and perform well rather than utilize this probability to dump high-cost personnel to the areas. The necessity for provisions to safeguard the offer of an HRA would not debar employees from obtaining market premium subsidies except if the HRA share made coverage certainly affordable. In conclusion, double-dipping really should not be allowable employees should have to choose from employer HRA-financed coverage and APTC, rather than receive both. Good results. These protections, as observed in current legislative plans (HR2911), a program that permits small employer assistance for coverage via HRAs could inspire some proprietors who would not then bid traditional select coverage to make it affordable for their employees.

Improving Network and Formulary Transparency

Increased network and formulary transparency would significantly increase the shopping experience of clients. Federal restrictions and the regulations in some states necessitate health strategies to make their network indexes and drug formularies obtainable online to upgrade them frequently. Thorough federal regulations, nevertheless, apply just to licensed health plans sold through the AQUI marketplaces, and express laws and restrictions do not apply to self-insured party health plans, which covers most employees insured through employee benefit plans. ERISA, which does cover employer plans, imposes less rigorous network disclosure requirements. Current statutes and regulations do not go far enough to confirm that insurers make available reliable provider directories and networks.

Transparent network coverage is necessary to make certain that consumers who enroll in narrow network plans understand the constraints they are accepting and can determine whether the providers they want or need are in-network. Propose development of a uniform rating system for disclosing the breadth or narrowness of provider networks. For example, McKinsey in its analysis of networks, defined broad networks as those with 70% of all hospitals in the rating area participating, narrow networks with 31% to 70% of all hospitals, and ultra-narrow networks with 30% or less of all hospitals participating. Ratings include the summaries of benefits and coverage that health care plans are required to give all enrollees and shoppers so that consumers can determine up front the breadth of the plan's network. Plans should describe the criteria used for determining network participation, the cost differentials for enrollees who use in- or out-of-network providers, and the balancing of bills.

Provider directories should be readily available online and in paper form. These must be easily searchable and understood by the general public. Consumers should be able to determine whether specific providers with whom they have established relationships, specific types of specialties that they need, providers in their geographic location, or providers who speak their language or accept patients, are available in a network before they sign up.

Directories for individual and small group plans should be available to the public online without the need to log-in or to provide a password. Insurers should provide directories for all individual market plans in a machine-readable form to permit private companies to generate search tools. Directories should legibly include information on providers, including name, location, niches, spoken languages, and if the set-up provider is accepting patients. Typically, private marketplace lookup tools potentially supplement the recently launched government facilitated marketplace medical doctor lookup tool. If providers are in a tiered network, the system must possess capabilities to search for providers by tier. The directory should obviously define the ramifications of tiered status in conditions comprehensible to ordinary consumers.

Consumers ought to be able to trust the accuracy of supplier directories. Directories should be updated monthly. A few states emphasize the accuracy of supplier directories as a requirement, although CMS recently requires monthly updates from QHPs in the federally facilitated marketplaces. If a directory erroneously lists a provider as participating or accepting patients, disenrollment becomes an option and allow enrollees to choose a different plan. express insurance regulators should file network listing updates, making network directory search part of their regular market research, as well as reply to complaints about directories. Trusted consumer organizations such as Consumers Union or Consumer Checkbook could rate plan networks for their comprehensiveness and quality.

Conclusion

ACA, passed by the members of the 111th U.S. Congress and later signed into law by President Barack Obama in the year 2010, benefited millions of Americans. Significantly, the legislature contains a widespread list of healthcare related provisions, whose objective at the time of its formation was to extend or offer coverage to millions of Americans who are uninsured. ACA achieved most of its objectives including the expansion of health care insurance access and protect people from overwhelming medical debts. However, the question asked is whether good intent makes providing health insurance any more manageable for small businesses while improving the health of Americans. The text demonstrates that for some small businesses, for instance, those with more than 50 employees, ACA enhanced premiums rates. However, some with young and healthy workers encountered premium hikes. Brokers and insurers quickly responded to these employer groups. Moreover, government policies allowed a wider variety of coverage options than ACA had originally envisioned

Despite the opposition and several adverse effects on small businesses and the healthcare industry, ACA deserves improvement rather than reapealing. While 32 states expanded Medicaid coverage to adults in low-income America since 2010, 19 states have not. As stated above, President Donald Trump made it clear that he would use all means necessary to get rid of Obamacare; seemingly to getting closer to accomplishing that wish. The main goal of ACA has been to lower the health care cost and denial of coverage to those with pre-existing conditions. The ACA accomplishes its goal. The same legislation's objective was to improve the efficiency of the system through the three primary goals discussed. Since its establishment in 2013, the Affordable Care Act has been at the center of contemplation and has had numerous impacts on small businesses Small Businesses in America. Therefore, the text included extensive discussion regarding the impacts of Obamacare on the healthcare organization from a business perspective; and the primary objectives pursued by ACA to make health insurance affordable as well as available, to people especially those from the low-income families. The Act provides consumers with different subsidies that lower the costs incurred in healthcare.

References

Altman, D. (2016). *The Affordable Care Act's little-noticed success: cutting the uninsured rate. Oct. 12, Kaiser Family Found., Menlo Park, CA.* Retrieved from https://www.kff.org/uninsured/perspective/the-affordable-care-acts-little-noticed-success-cutting-the-uninsured-rat.

Andorno, R. (2009). Human dignity and human rights as a common ground for global bioethics. *Journal of Medicine and Philosophy, 34*(3), 223-240. doi:10.1093/jmp/jhp023

Aristotle, A. (1962). *Nicomachean ethics. Translated by Martin Ostwald.* Englewood Cliffs, NJ: Prentice Hall.

Armstrong, D. (2010, November 17). *Health insurers iave $86 million to fight health law.* Retrieved from https://www.bloomberg.com/news/articles/2010-11-17/insurers-gave-u-s-chamber-86-million-used-to-oppose-obama-s-health-law

Ashley, B. M. & O' Rourkr, K. D. (1982). *Health care ethics: A theological analysis.* Washington, DC: Georgetown University Press.

Avery, K., Finegold, K., & Whitman, A. (2016). *Affordable Care Act has led to historic, widespread increase in health insurance coverage.* Department of Health and Human Services, Office of the Assistant Secretary for Planning and Evaluation. Retrieved from https://aspe.hhs.gov/system/files/pdf/207946/ACAHistoricIncreaseCoverage.pdf

Bassett, M. T. (2009). Bold steps for the health of Americans: Yes we can. *American Journal of Public Health, 99*, 587. doi:10.2105/AJPH.2009.159384

Beauchamp, T. L., & Childress, J. F. (2009). *Principles of biomedical ethics.* New York, NY: Oxford University Press.

Blumenthal, D., Abrams, M., & Nuzum, R. (2015). The affordable care act at 5 years. *New England Journal of Medicine, 372*(25) *doi*:10.1056/NEJMhpr1503614

Borelli, M. C., Bujanda, M., & Maier, K. (2016). The Affordable Care Act Insurance reforms: Where are we now, and what's next? *Clinical Diabetes, 34*(1), 58-64. doi:10.2337/diaclin.34.1.58

Brock, D. (1995). Public policy and bio ethics. In *Encyclopedia of Bioethics*. New York, NY: Macmillan Reference.

Buck, J. A. (2011). The looming expansion and transformation of public substance abuse treatment under the Affordable Care Act. *Health Affairs (Millwood)*; *30*, 1402-1410. doi:10.1377/hlthaff.2011.0480

Carman, K. G., & Eibner, C. (2014). Changes in health insurance enrollment since 2013: Evidence from the RAND Health Reform Opinion Study. *Rand Health Quarterly*, *4*(3). Retrieved from https://www.rand.org/pubs/research_reports/RR656.html.

Catlin, A. C., & Cowan, C. A. (2015). *History of health pending in the United States, 1960-2013*. Retrieved from https://www.cms.gov/...and...and.../NationalHealthExpendData/.../HistoricalNHEPaper

Center for Disease Control and Prevention (CDC). (2014). *Almost $500 million could be saved annually by making subsidized housing smoke-free. Sept. 9, CDC, Atlanta*. Retrieved from https://www.cdc.gov/media/releases/2014/p1002-smoke-free-housing.html

Center for Disease Control and Prevention (CDC). (2018). Public health preparedness and response 2018 National Snapshot. *U.S. Department of Health and Human Services*. Retrieved from https://www.cdc.gov/cpr/pubs-links/2018/documents/2018_Preparedness_Report.pdf

Chait, N., & Glied, S. (2018). Promoting prevention under the Affordable care act. *Annual Review of Public Health, 39*, 507-524. http://dx.doi.org/10.1146/annurev-publhealth-040617-013534

Chen, T. (2013). *Health insurance coverage and marriage behavior: Is there evidence of marriage-lock?* Retrieved from https://econ.uconn.edu/wp-content/uploads/sites/681/2017/02/marriage_lock_tianxu_chen_201701.pdf

Chernichovsky, D., & Leibowitz, A. A. (2010). Integrating public health and personal care in a reformed US health care system. *American Journal of Public Health, 100*(2), 205-211. doi:10.2105/AJPH.2008.156588

Chuang, C. H., Mitchell, J. L., Velott, D. L., Legro, R. S., Lehman, E. B., Confer, L., & Weisman, C. S. (2015). Women's awareness of their contraceptive benefits under the Patient Protection and Affordable Care Act. *American Journal of Public Health, 105*(S5), S713-S715. doi:10.2105/AJPH.2015.302829

Chung, S., Lesser, L. I., Lauderdale, D. S., Johns, N. E., Palaniappan, L. P., & Luft, H. S. (2015). Medicare annual preventive care visits: Use increased among fee-for-service patients, but many do not participate. *Health Affairs*, *34*(1), 11-20. http://dx.doi.org/10.1377/hlthaff.2014.0483

CNN. (2014, August 17). *CNN/ORC Poll*. Retrieved from http://i2cdn.turner.com/cnn/2014/images/08/08/re17g.pdf

Daniels, N. (1988). *Am I my parents' keepers?: An essay on justice between the young and the old*. Oxford, NY: Oxford University Press. doi:10.2307/2185582

Daniels, N. (2007). *Just health: Meeting health needs fairly*. Cambridge, UK: Cambridge University Press.

Daniels, N. (2008). Justice and access to health care. *Stanford Encyclopedia of Philosophy*. Retrieved from https://plato.stanford.edu/entries/justice-healthcareaccess/

Daniels, N., & Sabin, J. E. (2002). *Setting limits fairly: Can we learn to share medical resources?* Oxford, NY: Oxford University Press.

Dougherty, C. J. (1988). *American health care: realities, rights, and reforms*. New York, NY: Oxford University Press.

Emanuel, E. J., Grady, C. C., Crouch, R. A., Lie, R. K., Miller, F. G., & Wendler, D. D. (Eds.). (2008). *The Oxford textbook of clinical research ethics*. New York, NY: Oxford University Press.

Etheridge, E. W. (1992). *Sentinel for health: A history of the Centers for Disease Control*. Los Angeles, California: University of California Press.

Ewing, A. L. (2015). *The (unintended) Impact of the Affordable Care Act on divorce*. Retrieved from https://www.foxrothschild.com/publications/the-unintended-impact-of-the-affordable-care-act-on-divorce/

Farley, T. A. (2009). Reforming health care or reforming health? *America Journal of Public Health, 99*, 588–590. doi:10.2105/AJPH.2008.158808

Goldman, R. (2008). Woman divorces to afford life-saving surgery, *ABC News*. Retrieved from http://abcnews.go.com/Health/story?id=6402536&page=1

Goodman, A. (2009). President Obama's health plan and community-based prevention. *America Journal of Public Health, 99*, 1736–1738. doi:10.2105/AJPH.2009.174714

Graves, J. A., & Swartz, K. (2017). Effects of Affordable Care Act marketplaces and Medicaid eligibility expansion on access to cancer care. *Cancer Journal, 23*(3), 168. doi:10.1097/PPO.0000000000000260

Grossman, E. G., Sterkx, C. A., Blount, E. C., & Volberding, E. M. (2010). *Compilation of patient protection and Affordable Care Act*. Office of the legislative counsel, U.S. house of representatives. Retrieved from http://housedocs.house.gov/energycommerce/ppacacon.pdf

Haberkorn, J. (2012). Health policy briefs: The prevention and public health fund. *Health Affairs*. Retrieved from http://healthaffairs.org/healthpolicybriefs/brief_pdfs/healthpolicybrief_63.pdf

Hacker, J. S. (2001). *Medicare Plus: Increasing health coverage by expanding Medicare*. Retrieved from http://research.policyarchive.org/21867.pdf

Hall, K. S., Fendrick, A. M., Zochowski, M., & Dalton, V. K. (2014). Women's health and the Affordable Care Act: high hopes versus harsh realities? *American Journal of Public Health*, *104*(8), e10-e13. doi:10.2105/AJPH.2014.302045

Hamman, M. K., & Kapinos, K. A. (2015). Affordable Care Act provision lowered out-of-pocket cost and increased colonoscopy rates among men in Medicare. *Health Affairs*, *34*, 2069-2076. http://dx.doi.org/10.1377/hlthaff.2015.0571

Han, X., Yabroff, K. R., Guy Jr, G. P., Zheng, Z., & Jemal, A. (2015). Has recommended preventive service use increased after elimination of cost-sharing as part of the Affordable Care Act in the United States? *Preventive Medicine*, *78*, 85-91. http://dx.doi.org/10.1016/j.ypmed.2015.07.012

Immanuel Kant. (2010, May 20). *Stanford Encyclopedia of Philosophy*. Retrieved from https://plato.stanford.edu/entries/kant/

Kass, L. R. (1990). Practicing ethics: Where's the action? *Hastings Center Report*, *20*(1), 5-12. doi:10.2307/3562966

Katon, W. J., & Unützer, J. (2013). Health reform and the Affordable Care Act: The importance of mental health treatment to achieving the triple aim. *Journal of Psychosomatic Research*, *74*, 533-537. doi:10.1016/j.jpsychores.2013.04.005

Katz, J. (1984). *The silent world of doctor and patient*. Baltimore, MD: Johns Hopkins University Press.

Kelly, D., Magill, G., & Have, K. (2013). *Contemporary Catholic health care ethics*. Washington, DC: Georgetown University Press

Kirsch, R. (2003). *Will it be déjà u all over again?: Renewing the fight for health care for all*. Retrieved from http://www.fightingforourhealth.com/chapter/1-3/documents/2-Deja_Vu_Final.pdf

Koh, H. K., & Sebelius, K. G. (2010). Promoting prevention through the affordable care act. *New England Journal of Medicine, 363*, 1296-1299. doi:10.1056/NEJMp1008560

Kristof, N. (2009, August 29). Until medical bills do us part. *The New York Times*. Retrieved from https://www.nytimes.com/2009/08/30/opinion/30kristof.html

Lau, J. S., Adams, S. H., Park, M. J., Boscardin, W. J., & Irwin, C. E. (2014). Improvement in preventive care of young adults after the Affordable Care Act: The Affordable Care Act is helping. *The Journal of the American Medical Association (JAMA) Pediatrics, 168*, 1101-1106. doi:10.1001/jamapediatrics.2014.1691

Maclean, J. C., Pesko, M. F., & Hill, S. C. (2017). *The effect of insurance expansions on smoking cessation medication use: evidence from recent Medicaid expansions* (No. w23450). The National Bureau of Economic Research. doi:10.3386/w23450

Madison, K., Schmidt, H., & Volpp, K. G. (2013). Smoking, obesity, health insurance, and health incentives in the Affordable Care Act. *The Journal of the American Medical Association, 310*(2), 143-144. doi:10.1001/jama.2013.7617

Manchikanti, L., Helm, S. I., Benyamin, R. M., & Hirsch, J. A. (2017). A critical analysis of Obamacare: Affordable care or insurance for many and coverage for few? *Pain Physician, 20*, 111-138. Retrieved from http://www.painphysicianjournal.com/current/pdf?article=NDMwMg%3D%3D&journal=104

Markit, I. H. S. (2017). *The complexities of physician supply and demand: Projections from 2015 to 2030*. Retrieved from https://aamc-black.global.ssl.fastly.net/production/media/filer_public/85/d7/85d7b689-f417-4ef0-97fbecc129836829/aamc_2018_workforce_projections_update_april_11_2018.pdf

McAfee, T., Davis, K. C., Alexander Jr, R. L., Pechacek, T. F., & Bunnell, R. (2013). Effect of the first federally funded US antismoking national media campaign. *The Lancet, 382*, 2003-2011. doi:10.1016/S0140-6736(13)61686-4

Navarro, M. (2016, November 30). U.S. will ban smoking in public housing nationwide. *New York Times*. Retrieved from https://www.nytimes.com/2016/11/30/nyregion/us-will-ban-smoking-in-public-housing-nationwide.html

Powers, M., & Faden, R. (2006). *Social justice: The moral foundations of public health and health policy*. New York, New York: Oxford Press.

Price, C. C., & Saltzman, E. (2013). The economic impact of the Affordable

Care Act on Arkansas. *Rand Health Quarterly, 3*(1), 1. Retrieved from https://www.rand.org/pubs/research_reports/RR157.html

Rawls, J. (1971). *A theory of justice*. Cambridge, MA: Belknap Press / Harvard University Press.

Rigby, E. (2011). How the National Prevention Council can overcome key challenges and improve Americans' health. *Health Affairs, 30*, 2149-2156. doi:10.1377/hlthaff.2011.0718

Rigby, E., Clark, J. H., & Pelika, S. (2014). Party politics and enactment of "Obamacare": A policy-centered analysis of minority party involvement. *Journal of Health Politics, Policy, and Law, 39*(1), 57-95. doi:10.1215/03616878-2395181

Rojas, S.L, Amico, P., Goode, S., Hoerger, T., Jacobs, S., & Renaud, J. (2016). Evaluation of the health care innovation awards: community resource planning, prevention, and monitoring. second annual report. *Research Triangle Park, NC: RTI Int.* Retrieved from https://downloads.cms.gov/files/cmmi/hcia-communityrppm-secondevalrpt.pdf

Roy, A. (2011). How the heritage foundation, a conservative think tank, promoted the individual mandate. *Forbes (Pharma and Healthcare)*. Retrieved from https://www.forbes.com/sites/theapothecary/2011/10/20/how-a-conservative-think-tank-invented-the-individual-mandate/#44a208636187

RTI Int. (2016). *State Innovation Models (SIM) initiative evaluation: Model test year two annual report* (RTI International CMS Contract No. HHSM-500-2014-00037i). Baltimore, MD: Centers for Medicare & Medicaid Services. Retrieved from https://downloads.cms.gov/files/cmmi/sim-round-2test-secondannrpt.pdf

Ruger, J. P. (2010). *Health and social justice*. New York, NY: Oxford University Press.

Sabik, L. M., & Adunlin, G. (2017). The ACA and cancer screening and diagnosis. *Cancer Journal, 23*(3), 151. doi:10.1097/PPO.0000000000000261

Sander L. M. (1990, July 2). *H.R.4449-101st Congress (1989-1990): Patient Self Determination Act of 1990*. Retrieved from https://www.congress.gov/bill/101st-congress/house-bill/4449

Shartzer, A., Long, S. K., & Anderson, N. (2015). Access to care and affordability have improved following Affordable Care Act implementation; problems remain. *Health Affairs, 35*(1), 161-168. doi:10.1377/hlthaff.2015.0755

Simon, K., Soni, A., & Cawley, J. (2017). The impact of health insurance on preventive care and health behaviors: evidence from the first two years of the ACA Medicaid expansions. *Journal of Policy Analysis and Management, 36,* 390-417. doi:10.1002/pam.21972

Skopec, L., & Sommers, B. D. (2013). *Seventy-one million additional Americans are receiving preventive services coverage without cost-sharing under the Affordable Care Act.* Retrieved from https://aspe.hhs.gov/.../ seventy-one-million-additional-americans-are-receiving-preven.

Skopec, L., Waidmann, T.A., Sung, J., & Dean, O. (2016). *Monitoring the impact of health reform on americans ages 50–64: Access to health care improved during early ACA marketplace implementation.* AARP Public policy institute. Retrieved from https://www.aarp.org/content/dam/aarp/ppi/2015/access-to-health-care-improved-during-early-aca-%20marketplace-implementation. PDF

Slusky, D., & Ginther, D. (2017). Did Medicaid expansion reduce medical divorce? (No. w23139). *The National Bureau of Economic Research.* doi:10.3386/w23139

Sobel, L., Salganicoff, A., Kurani, N., & Wiens, J. (2015). *Coverage of contraceptive services: A review of health insurance plans in five states.* Menlo Park, CA: Henry J. Kaiser Family Foundation. Retrieved from http://files.kff.org/ attachment/report-coverage-of-contraceptive-services-a-review-of-health-insurance-plans-in-five-states

Sommers, B. D., Blendon, R. J., Orav, E. J., & Epstein, A. M. (2016). Changes in utilization and health among low-income adults after Medicaid expansion or expanded private insurance. *The Journal of the American Medical Association (JAMA) Internal Medicine, 176,* 1501-1509. doi:10.1001/ jamainternmed.2016.4419

Sonfield, A., Tapales, A., Jones, R. K., & Finer, L. B. (2015). Impact of the federal contraceptive coverage guarantee on out-of-pocket payments for contraceptives: 2014 update. *Contraception, 91,* 44–48. doi:10.1016/j. contraception.2014.09.006

Sung, J., Skopec, L., & Wadmann, T. A. (2015, May 17). Monitoring the impact of health reform on Americans. Pages 50–64. *AARP Public policy institute.* Retrieved from https://www.aarp.org/content/dam/aarp/ppi/2015/ monitoring-impact-of-health-reform-may.pdf

Tal, B. (2012). Capitalizing on the Upcoming Infrastructure Stimulus. *CIBC World Markets* Retrieved from: http://research.cibcwm.com/economic_public/download/occrept66.pdf

The Bellagio study group on child survival. (2003). Knowledge into action for child survival. *The Lancet, 362*, 323-327. doi:10.1016/S0140-6736(03)13977-3

The Henry Kaiser Family Foundation (KFF). (2011). *Kaiser health tracking poll.* Retrieved from http://kaiserfamilyfoundation.files.wordpress.com/2013/01/8166-c.pdf.

The Henry Kaiser Family Foundation (KFF). (2013a). *The Affordable Care Act three years post-enactment. Issue Brief.* Retrieved from https://kaiserfamilyfoundation.files.wordpress.com/2013/04/84291.pdf

The Henry Kaiser Family Foundation (KFF). (2016). *Uninsured: Key facts about the uninsured population.* Retrieved from http://www.kff.org/uninsured/keyfactsabouttheuninsured

The Henry Kaiser Family Foundation (KFF). (2018). *Status of State Action on the Medicaid Expansion Decision.* Retrieved from https://www.kff.org/health-reform/state-indicator/state-activity-around-expanding-medicaid-under-the-affordable-care-act

The Kaiser Family Foundation and Health Research & Educational Trust. (2013b). *Employer health benefits annual survey.* Retrieved from https://kaiserfamilyfoundation.files.wordpress.com/2012/09/8465-employer-health-benefits-2013.pdf

The New York Times. (2012, March 25). *Results of The New York Times/CBS news poll.* Retrieved from http://www.nytimes.com/interactive/2012/03/27/us/03272012_polling_doc.html

Wallace, J., & Sommers, B. D. (2015). Effect of dependent coverage expansion of the Affordable Care Act on health and access to care for young adults. *The Journal of the American Medical Association (JAMA) Pediatrics, 169*, 495-497. doi:10.1001/jamapediatrics.2014.3574

Williams, E. D., & Redhead, C. S. (2010). *Public health, workforce, quality, and related provisions in the Patient Protection and Affordable Care Act (PPACA).* CRS Report for Congress. Washington, DC: Congress. Research. Service, Library of. Congress. Retrieved from https://www.aamc.org/download/130996/data/pdf

About the Author

Dr. Ivan Salaberrios resides in Pickerington, Ohio. Dr. Ivan holds several accredited degrees; a Bachelor of Technical management Science (BS) in Management from DeVry University; a Master of Business Administration (MBA) from Keller Graduate School; and a Doctor of Business Administration (DBA) from Walden University. Dr. Ivan also is a certified Project Management Professional (PMP) and Lean Six Sigma Black Belt Certified

Dr. Ivan is the CEO and founder of AIM Technical Consultants. His career in the telecommunications industry began as a field engineer working with AMPs Radio Equipment, where he obtained extensive experience in RF Engineering, Network Engineering and Project Management.

In 17 years, Dr. Ivan has grown AIM from a handful of engineers to one of the largest staffing and engineering firms focused exclusively in wireless telecom. This growth is largely attributable to Ivan's relationship-building skills, dedication to exceptional service delivery, and unwavering focus on continuous improvement. Dr. Ivan is a Gulf War veteran, serving an enlistment term in the U.S. Navy on the USS *Yorktown* CG-48. He was honorably discharged in 1992.

To reach Dr. Ivan Salaberrios for information on consulting or doctoral coaching, please **e-mail: ivans@aimtechinc.com**

www.ingramcontent.com/pod-product-compliance
Lightning Source LLC
Chambersburg PA
CBHW060608200326
41521CB00007B/706